Changing the Law
A Practical Guide to Law Reform

Commonwealth Secretariat

 The Commonwealth

 **Commonwealth Association of Law Reform Agencies**

Commonwealth Secretariat
Marlborough House
Pall Mall
London SW1Y 5HX
United Kingdom

Published by the Commonwealth Secretariat
Edited by Prepress Projects Ltd
Typeset by Nova Techset Private Limited, Bengaluru & Chennai, India
Cover design by Commonwealth Secretariat
Printed by Charlesworth Press, Wakefield

Copies of this publication may be obtained from

Publications Section
Commonwealth Secretariat
Marlborough House
Pall Mall
London SW1Y 5HX
United Kingdom
Tel: +44 (0)20 7747 6534
Email: publications@commonwealth.int
Web: www.thecommonwealth.org/publications

A catalogue record for this publication is available from the British Library.

ISBN (paperback): 978-1-84929-174-3
ISBN (e-book): 978-1-84859-966-6

The Commonwealth Office of Civil and Criminal Justice Reform supports Commonwealth countries in delivering access to justice and sustainable development through the creation of fair and effective national laws.

occjr@commonwealth.int

Foreword

The Rt Hon Patricia Scotland QC
Secretary-General of the Commonwealth

In 2015, the global Sustainable Development Goals included the principle that the development aspirations of all people everywhere are intimately linked with the promotion of the rule of law. While this depends on many factors, at a fundamental level the rule of law depends on the quality of the laws that are made and upheld. That is, the rule of law requires good law. Law reform is the process that makes law good, and good law better. Institutions and systems that provide fair, modern and cost-effective law reform underpin the rule of law, and therefore serve an important role in delivering sustainable development.

It is for these reasons that the Commonwealth Secretariat has for many years supported national law reform efforts. Our recently launched Commonwealth Office of Civil and Criminal Justice Reform will carry forward this work by making available for use by all Commonwealth member countries legal tools, knowledge and good practice manuals – such as this guide. Our objective in doing so is to strengthen the rule of law, and to facilitate swift and equitable access to justice for all.

In matters of law and law reform, as in everything else, there is considerable diversity within the Commonwealth. There are, however, many common threads that run through this diversity and connect most, if not all, Commonwealth jurisdictions. Regardless of similarities and differences, all Commonwealth countries stand to benefit from the accumulated practical wisdom generously shared in these pages.

The Commonwealth Secretariat is indebted to our principal partner in this venture, the Commonwealth Association of Law Reform Agencies, and to the many others who have contributed. The outcome of our collaboration, this guide to law reform, will help us all to meet our Commonwealth Charter commitment to upholding the rule of law as an essential protection for all the people of the Commonwealth.

Foreword

The Hon Philip Cummins AM
President of the Commonwealth Association of Law Reform Agencies

To sustain the rule of law, law reform needs to be principled, based on sound methods, and to take full account of the views of civil society and of experts. It should be respected, reliable, rigorous and responsive.

Experience and specialist knowledge are needed when seeking to deliver law reform that is successful by these measures. This guide provides practical guidance on the day-to-day process of carrying out law reform in any jurisdiction. Much has been written about law reform, but this guide is the first to have a practical and multi-jurisdictional focus. The need for such a guide has been widely acknowledged.

The guide takes the reader in a very practical way through a typical law reform project. It aims to be accessible and engaging, whether read as a whole or referred to when questions arise. The guide sets out the stages of a project, providing ideas and discussing practical options. It suggests the advantages of different approaches, explaining the reasons and providing examples.

The guide is intended for all those involved in law reform in any capacity, including within dedicated law reform agencies, as well as within government ministries and agencies. There will also be particular benefits if this guide serves to stimulate interest in and support for high-quality law reform in jurisdictions where reform is currently given low priority.

The Commonwealth Association of Law Reform Agencies and its members have long hoped and planned for the production of such a guide. Together with the Commonwealth Secretariat, we are proud to present this guide to law reform. As a significant undertaking, it has been written with assistance from a wide variety of contributors, including many experienced law reformers from across the Commonwealth and beyond. The experience from this range of jurisdictions will enable countries to learn from each other. Our association is grateful to the Secretariat for working with us to produce this guide. It has been an effective and valuable partnership – with, we hope, significant benefits to law reform.

Acknowledgements

This guide was produced by the Governance and Peace Directorate of the Commonwealth Secretariat, jointly with the Commonwealth Association of Law Reform Agencies.

Editor: Richard Percival, Senior Research Fellow, Law Reform and Policy Analysis, Cardiff Law School.

Associate Editor: Michael Sayers, former Chief Executive, Law Commission for England and Wales, and Hon General Secretary of Commonwealth Association of Law Reform Agencies.

Commonwealth Secretariat team: Steven Malby, Head, Office of Civil and Criminal Justice Reform; Segametsi Mothibatsela, Legal Adviser; and Matthew Moorhead, Legal Adviser.

Serving members and staff of many law reform agencies have assisted with the drafting and revision of this guide, along with others. The Commonwealth Association of Law Reform Agencies and the Commonwealth Secretariat are most grateful to all of them, and thank them most warmly. They are mainly members of the Commonwealth Association of Law Reform Agencies. They include the main authors, listed below, who drafted sections of the guide, those from different jurisdictions, who commented on the drafts – and especially the Editor, assisted by the Associate Editor.

Alberta Law Reform Institute
    Peter Lown QC (former Director)

Australian Law Reform Commission
    Professor Rosalind Croucher AM (former President)

Bangladesh Law Commission

British Columbia Law Institute

Cayman Islands Law Reform Commission

Law Commission for England and Wales
    Tamara Goriely and Vindelyn Hilman-Smith

Ghana Law Reform Commission

Law Reform Commission of Hong Kong
    Stuart Stoker (formerly the Secretary)

Law Reform Commission of Ireland
  Raymond Byrne

Legal Reform Department, Ministry of Justice, Jamaica
  Maurice Bailey

Kenya Law Reform Commission

Law Reform Commission of Mauritius
  Pierre Rosario Domingue

Law Reform and Development Commission of Namibia
  Yvonne Dausab, Felicity Owoses and Robert Xamseb

New Zealand Law Commission

Scottish Law Commission
  Malcolm McMillan

South African Law Reform Commission

Samoa Law Reform Commission

Law Reform Commission of Tanzania
  Aloysius Mujulizi

Law Reform Commission of Trinidad and Tobago

Uganda Law Reform Commission
  Vastina Ruki-Nsanze

Victorian Law Reform Commission

Contents

Contents

Chapter 1

Introduction

Chapter 1
Introduction

Law is always in need of reform. To be successful, law reform must be of a high standard. This guide is designed to provide practical assistance to users seeking to deliver high-standard law reform outcomes. Using examples and experience from around the Commonwealth and beyond, it guides users through each of the phases of a successful reform. It is the first general guide to conducting law reform in Commonwealth countries.

The need for law reform has been widely recognised for many years. Law reform activity has grown, in a great variety of ways and with varying success. In order to enhance justice and legal efficiency, and contribute to socio-economic development, reform needs to be of a high standard. Across the Commonwealth, there is a need for information and guidance about the different ways in which law reform can be undertaken, learning from the various methods that have proved successful in Commonwealth jurisdictions.

1.1 The purpose of this guide

There are at least 60 law reform agencies in the Commonwealth, and a good number outside the Commonwealth. In addition, in some jurisdictions, law reform is performed through a range of other means.

Law reform has become ever more demanding. Public expectations have increased, and pressures have grown. Law commissioners and the staff of law reform agencies often move on swiftly. In addition, law reform agencies have increased in number and continue to do so: the newer agencies tend to be in small states, and tend themselves to be smaller.

Until now, there has been no general guidance on how to carry out law reform in Commonwealth countries. This guide fills that gap. It is simply a guide and is not prescriptive.

Law reformers themselves will benefit from such guidance, as well as others involved in law reform in other ways.

This guide is for:

- those with experience in law reform within law reform agencies and government ministries;

- those who are new to being closely involved in law reform, such as new law reform agencies, new members of staff and new law commissioners and board members, and others coming for the first time to law reform, such as those conducting one-off reviews of specific subjects;

- the recipients of law reform outputs, particularly in government and in legislatures; and

- governments and others considering the possible establishment of a new law reform agency, to assist them with fully understanding typical models and processes.

The guide is relevant across the Commonwealth, and indeed beyond. It may, however, be of particular relevance to developing Commonwealth countries, as well as small Commonwealth jurisdictions.

The guide is of an entirely practical nature. It aims to assist a law reformer at their desk, with ideas about how to progress a particular law reform project, from start to finish.

Throughout, points are illustrated with examples from around the Commonwealth and beyond. The examples are drawn from a wide range of law reform agencies (and others). Examples from some agencies recur, with the aim of providing a sense of how particular practices build upon each other in the distinct processes used by these law reform agencies. The examples are chosen to illustrate points covered in each chapter. However, they will frequently also provide outlines of the substance of the law reform under consideration by the agency responsible. The aim of this is to give some idea of both what law reform agencies around the world have sought to improve and how they have gone about doing it.

The guide explains a variety of approaches to the elements of the law reform process, discussing their advantages and disadvantages as appropriate. Not all will be relevant or practical for all law reformers. The guide is intended to be used selectively, and to be capable of adaptation to different contexts.

The guide also provides suggestions and options for law reformers who have few resources, including tailored coverage of agencies in small states and jurisdictions. At the same time, it covers some relatively sophisticated procedures which will be appropriate for better funded or larger law reform agencies.

1.2 The approach of the guide

The guide broadly seeks to follow law reform processes through each stage, from the initiation of projects to their final implementation.

The guide starts with an account of law reform and law reformers. Chapter 2 seeks to explore the nature of law reform as it has developed over the last 50 years. The chapter goes on to consider how law reform legislation fits into the legislative scheme in general, and then surveys the key features of law reform agencies and their values. In this connection, it considers the nuanced way in which law reform agencies relate to governments. It provides a characterisation of the models that presently exist – the standard model of a statutory law reform agency; the institute model at sub-state level in Canada and Australia; and the in-government unit. When the guide uses the term 'law reform agency', it refers to all three of these models.

Chapter 3 looks at how law reform projects or inquiries are initiated. The starting point is the mandate – statutory or otherwise – of the agency, which is usually very broad. It then looks at how an agency can select types of projects, and discusses the advantages and disadvantages of each. Under the theme of relations with government, it looks at the ways in which a law reform agency receives or decides upon work, whether in references from government or in programmes of work generated by the agency itself (albeit usually approved by government). The chapter also looks at the institutionalisation of relations with governments as an integral part of the initiation process. The selection criteria for law reform projects are then considered. Finally, the chapter looks at how law reform fits the contemporary context, as well as some of the current challenges to law reform.

Chapter 4 considers the planning and management of projects. It starts by looking at how project teams are formed, and then considers the basic elements of project management – a timeline and a budget; evaluation of progress; co-ordination of inputs; and risk management. The chapter goes on to discuss key mechanisms for project management. These include task lists, and the identification of responsibilities, dependencies and timelines.

Chapter 5 considers the first stage of a law reform project – the research and drafting in the period before the start of consultation. A variety of first stage documents are examined, including documents that provide background, analysis and initial questions or conclusions for consultation. The chapter considers legal research, as practised in law reform agencies. This means not only research into the law, and its development within the jurisdiction, but also comparative legal research and empirical social science research. The chapter then considers the nature and value of pre-consultation engagement with stakeholders. It provides guidance on the drafting of consultation documents and the development of legal policy in a consultation document, as well as the balance between provisional proposals and questions.

Chapter 6 addresses the role of consultation as a definitive element of law reform. Following a discussion of why consultation is important, the chapter considers different forms of consultation process. It goes on to discuss the identification of the audience for consultation and the publication process. The chapter then looks at active consultation – how law reform agencies reach out to the communities with which they aim to engage through advisory groups, meetings and events, and observational consultation and site visits. It underlines the importance of record keeping. It examines the persistent problem of difficult-to-reach interests – how do law reform agencies reach out to those communities that are not organised in such a way as to be readily accessible to the law reformer? Finally, the chapter considers some of the practical issues in relation to written responses, such as time extensions and confidentiality.

Chapter 7 turns to policy-making after consultation. It considers how the fruits of consultation are analysed, understood and fed into the policy-making process, leading law reform agencies to come to conclusions. The chapter looks at the development of documents by which law reform project teams come to recommendations for final decisions, and how those are approved within a law reform agency. The chapter then turns to the advantages and disadvantages of cost–benefit analysis as a tool for law reformers, and considers other forms of (usually) government-inspired assessments that a law reform agency may be expected to produce, or may or may not wish to perform itself. Finally, the chapter looks at how those law reform agencies that produce draft bills with their reports go about doing so.

Chapter 8 covers the last stage in a law reform project – publication, implementation and following up a report. The chapter starts by considering the very real challenge of the implementation of law reform agencies' reports. It looks at the process of publication and a government's response. The chapter goes on to consider and discuss how law reform agencies can support governments in implementing recommendations after they have been finally reported. This involves the consideration of possible avenues of influence, such as various forms of engagement with government and the role of supportive interest groups. Finally, the chapter considers the development in a small number of jurisdictions of a special parliamentary process for law reform agency bills, and discusses whether or not the model could be more widely used.

Chapters 9 and 10 address cross-cutting issues in law reform for Commonwealth countries. Chapter 9 discusses the impact of standards and international obligations on law reform processes, including international human rights law. It also introduces the 2030 Agenda for Sustainable Development and explores the important contribution that law reform can make to the realisation of the Sustainable Development Goals. Chapter 10 turns to the particular challenges of law reform in small Commonwealth states and jurisdictions. Of the 52 members of the Commonwealth, 30 are classified as small states. In addition, law reform agencies exist in a number of non-state jurisdictions such as Jersey and the Cayman Islands. Chapter 10 covers the challenges and advantages of a small population and land area, and the impact that can have on the structure of law reform agencies in small states and jurisdictions, including the particular pressures on staffing. The chapter looks at how small state and jurisdiction agencies adapt the law reform process, and the particular significance of comparative research for them. It goes on to outline how, despite the challenges, small state and jurisdiction law reform agencies have made very considerable contributions to the law. Finally, the chapter assesses the particular utility of co-operation between law reform agencies, including through regional associations, and small state and jurisdiction agencies.

Chapter 2

Law Reform and Law Reformers

Chapter 2
Law Reform and Law Reformers

Chapter 2 explores the nature of law reform as it has developed over the past 50 years. The chapter goes on to consider how law reform legislation fits into the legislative scheme in general, and then surveys the key features of law reform agencies and their values. In this connection, it considers the nuanced way in which law reform agencies and governments have separate roles. It provides a characterisation of the institutional models that presently exist – the standard model of a statutory law reform agency; the institute model sometimes used at sub-state level in Canada and Australia; and the in-government unit.

2.1 What is law reform?

The law is constantly changing. The business of government includes legislating in pursuance of political and policy goals. Very often, and quite properly, government terms its political and policy objectives 'reform'. Legislating for government reform is the very substance of everyday political work in democracies throughout the world. However, the sort of reform that requires changes to the law is not what is meant in this guide by 'law reform'.

Law reform as an activity, and law reform agencies as institutions, are conceptually intertwined.

Rather, 'law reform' is used to refer to the principal, although not the only, activity of bodies, such as law reform commissions, law institutes, and other law reform agencies and entities that are dedicated to changing the law. While there is no single accepted definition of law reform as an activity, broadly, law reform means improving the substance of the law in significant ways.

This key characteristic of law reform distinguishes it from a number of related processes, some of which may also be undertaken by some law reform agencies.

Law reform is a process that is distinct, for example, from the *revision* or *consolidation* of laws. The term 'law revision' is normally used to refer to statutory amendments that make no change at all to the substance of the law. They make the law more accessible and simpler to understand, but without changing its meaning. *Law reform is about substance, while law revision and consolidation are about form.* Consolidation, in particular, is the bringing together of statute law in a number of different instruments into a single, new, legislative instrument. Consolidation re-packages, but does not substantively change, the law. There may be some scope to change the language of the law, or make the most minor and technical changes to its effect, for instance to avoid absurdity. But the fundamental objective is to have a neutral impact on the substance of the law. 'Consolidation' and 'law revision' are almost synonyms, used in different places to refer to much the same process.

Law reform is about the substance of the law. It means improving the law in significant ways.

In some jurisdictions, 'revision' is reserved for the wholesale consolidation of the laws of the jurisdiction, undertaken as a single exercise. In some Commonwealth jurisdictions, consolidation or revision are functions conferred on law reform agencies. In many, these functions are undertaken by the office responsible for legislative drafting, or a unit dedicated to the task elsewhere within government.

There is another, slightly different sense in which the word 'revision' is used. In a small number of jurisdictions, the law reform agency is charged with publishing as-amended versions of Acts. The Law Revision Department of the Uganda Law Reform Commission publishes from time to time the complete Revised Edition of the Laws of Uganda; that is, the full text of all the primary legislation of Uganda in its amended form.[1] As with pure consolidation, these functions do not change the substance of the law. Similarly, in the Republic of Ireland, the Law Reform Commission of Ireland is responsible for publishing revised Acts; that is, administrative consolidations of Acts in their amended form since 2006 (plus some earlier Acts). These Revised Acts are not enacted by the Parliament of Ireland, and therefore do not have any formal or official status, but they have been cited with approval in the courts.[2]

Some law reform agencies also undertake projects to repeal obsolete legislation. Only statutes that have no possible application are proposed for repeal, so again this activity does not change the law. A much more ambitious version of this is undertaken in South Africa, where the Law Reform Commission has been engaged for a number of years in a wide-ranging statutory law revision project to review all of South African national legislation in order to determine whether some or all of its provisions are obsolete, spent or otherwise incompatible with the South African Constitution.[3]

Consolidation, revision and the repeal of obsolete statutes are all functions of some law reform agencies, but they are to be distinguished from law reform proper. The term 'law reform' is sometimes used more broadly to include all of the functions of law reform agencies. However, this guide focuses on the distinct main task of law reform agencies of examining existing laws and where appropriate advocating for or implementing changes in law. Tasks such as law consolidation or revision are touched upon only insofar as a law reform agency will take into account its whole range of functions in setting up its work programme, planning its activities and assessing its use of resources.

This main function, to which the guide largely confines the use of the term 'law reform' (or sometimes 'substantive law reform'), can be distinguished from consolidation/revision and repeal of dead statutes, because its key objective is to change, and thereby improve, the substantive law.

In this regard, *codification* of law is often included within the scope of law reform. Codification has been described, by the Law Commission for England and Wales' founding Chair, Lord Scarman, as:

> *...a species of enacted law which purports so to formulate the law that it becomes within its field the authoritative, comprehensive and exclusive source of that law. It is, however, distinct from consolidation, in that it allows for and indeed generally requires that the brought-together law be at the same time improved. It is a method of law reform proper, rather than a distinct, free-standing objective. Within common law legal systems, codification may involve both the bringing together of provisions in a number of statutes, and the re-framing of common law rules in statutory form.[4]*

Codification was a major preoccupation for the British law commissions in their earlier years. It now takes a less central

Law reform is distinct from the revision or consolidation of the law, which are about the form of the law.

place, although codification still exercises a strong pull in the criminal context. The Law Commission for England and Wales[5] is currently engaged in a codification of sentencing procedure.

The founding statute of the Law Commission for England and Wales and the Scottish Law Commission was the Law Commissions Act 1965. Just as those commissions became the model for many law reform agencies, the words of that Act have frequently been used elsewhere. The 'functions' of the Commissions are set out in section 3. Section 3(1) comprises mostly a list of obligations and techniques (such as comparative research), but its opening words are:

> It shall be the duty of each of the Commissions to take and keep under review all the law with which they are respectively concerned with a view to its systematic development and reform, including in particular the codification of such law, the elimination of anomalies, the repeal of obsolete and unnecessary enactments, the reduction of the number of separate enactments and generally the simplification and modernisation of the law.

Law reform, then, was originally conceived as including the reviewing of the law; and its general touchstones were seen as 'simplification and modernisation'.

Neither of those on its own functions to distinguish law reform from political legislation, but they do give a flavour of law reform. Generally, law reform at least starts with the state of the law as its subject matter, rather than a social, political or economic problem independently defined. In addition, what it seeks to improve is the law. The impetus to do so may very well be motivated by social or other concerns, but the law remains the central focus of law reform.

All legislative action is fundamentally political, but law reform agencies are non-political in the sense of being outside the competition of ideas between political parties.

One way in which law reform distinguishes itself from that which is done by governments is insisting that it is not political. Indeed, the non-political nature of law reform is universally seen as fundamental by law reform agencies. In a wide social science sense, all policy-making is 'political' in that it involves 'the authoritative allocation of values' or is a decision 'which confirms, allocates, or shifts power'.[6]

However, law reform agencies are non-political in the sense that they do not engage in work that would appear to take sides in the competition of ideas between political parties that exists in functioning democracies.

This does not mean that law reform must be *non-controversial*. Much of law reform occasions public controversy, at least among some parts of the public. It is indeed rare that, for instance, substantive proposals in the criminal sphere do not do so. However, it cannot be directly driven by party political controversy – that is, something supported by one of the main parties in the state and opposed by another.

Furthermore, there are some legal subjects that fall outside the reach of law reform. Taxation is provided for through legislation, but it is generally considered outside the scope of a law reform agency's remit to examine whether the rate of corporate or income tax should be 'reformed' by way of an increase or decrease. In some states, legislation provides for membership of a military alliance, or the constitution requires neutrality. These similarly are not matters for law reform.

As will be seen in the next chapter, most law reform agencies' criteria for undertaking law reform projects include that it be 'suitable' for law reform. Expanding that criterion, relevant questions include: is the project suitable for a non-political body of lawyers? A key feature of law reform is that it is generally an activity undertaken and led by lawyers.

Whether or not a topic is suitable for law reform is a key question. Suitable topics tend to be areas or activities undertaken and led by lawyers.

As such, a general characterisation of law reform is that it is a non-partisanly political form of (legal) policy formation, which is within the professional capacity of lawyers to accomplish.

It will be apparent that law reform agencies as institutions and law reform as an activity are conceptually intertwined. Law reform is what law reform agencies do; and law reform agencies are (mainly) there to do law reform.

During the 50-year history of law reform agencies, different areas of law have come under law reform examination at different times. The following is a flavour of the issues that one or more law reform agencies have considered during that time:

- reform of family law to take account of changing family relationships;
- reform of civil liability law, such as the extent of the duties of occupiers of property;
- reform of aspects of commercial law, including consumer protection law;
- reform of law on ownership of land (real property) and transfer of ownership (conveyancing);

- reform of court processes generally, including mass claims ('class actions');

- use of alternative dispute resolution;

- the right to privacy, including freedom from intrusion by the media and, separately, freedom from surveillance by the state;

- protection of persons whose decision-making capacity may be in question, and other vulnerable persons;

- criminal law, such as conspiracy and homicide law, or procedural issues, such as double jeopardy and corporate criminal liability;

- the regulation of assisted human reproduction;

- the scope of the use of DNA in a forensic setting and (sometimes later) the development and scope of a DNA database; and

- the regulation of harmful digital communications, notably on social media.

Some of these involve the review of matters that may not have attracted political priority and are therefore matters that a law reform agency is well suited to address, while others will have arisen after the establishment of most law reform agencies. It is therefore clear that the scope of projects that a law reform agency may be required to review will alter with the passage of time: the contemporary setting will often identify at least one project that may not have been an issue in previous years.

Throughout this guide, practical examples of specific law reform projects are used to illustrate the procedural process of law reform with reference to particular changes to the law proposed by law reform agencies.

2.2 Who does law reform?

The function of law reform can be carried out in a variety of ways. Each jurisdiction chooses a forum and process for law reform that is appropriate in its own context, taking into account issues such as the availability of resources and expertise.

The starting point for law reform in modern times, however, has been the institutional development over the last 50 years of a distinct form: the law reform agency. This is the predominant approach within the Commonwealth, and in some other common law countries. A law reform agency comprises a standing and independent body established in order to provide recommendations and advice on law reform. Such bodies have been established in both large and small jurisdictions, in unitary and federal states, and at the sub-state level.

Over time, two families of models of law reform agencies have developed. The first, and most widespread, is what is now regarded as the 'classic' or standard model: the establishment of an independent law reform body by statute. Secondly, the 'institute' model consists of the setting up of an independent body by agreement between leading legal interests and stakeholders.

Some arrangements, however, do not fit into either of these categories. A small number of jurisdictions have established other methods. For example, especially in a small jurisdiction, a government may arrange for a ministry to take the lead on law reform. This may be the ministry of justice or the office of the attorney-general. Although not independent of government, such law reform agencies tend to broadly adopt the methods and approaches of an independent law reform agency. Such a unit is therefore to be distinguished from, say, the section in a ministry of justice that is responsible for civil law as a policy area, just as another section may be responsible for court administration or judges' pensions.

In the Commonwealth, much law reform is undertaken by independent law reform agencies. There are other arrangements in some Commonwealth jurisdictions, such as using one-off committees or working within government.

Jamaica: Law reform within government

Jamaica has a system in place by which law reform functions, both making recommendations and implementing them, are carried out by the Legal Reform Department, being a department of the Jamaica Government's Ministry of Justice.

The Legal Reform Department began in 1973 as a division of the Ministry of Justice, and later was given departmental status.

The mandate of this department is:

> To keep under review the laws applicable in Jamaica with a view to its systematic reform to meet the changing needs of the Jamaican society, and to assist in the implementation of law reform proposals in accordance with Government policy.

The Legal Reform Department also undertakes additional duties to support the law reform process.

Alternatively, from time to time, governments may set up a one-off committee or commission, or ask an individual, to consider a particular issue and to provide recommendations for reform of the law to ministers. Where the issues to be addressed are legal in nature, a judge or senior lawyer (such as a Queen's Counsel or equivalent) is often appointed to carry out the review or as the chair of a review team. The reviewer, or committee or commission, makes its report to ministers on the issue and at that point has fulfilled its remit.

Such review mechanisms are not undertaken by standing or established agencies or bodies. Some reviews are however carried out by a process similar to that adopted by a law reform agency for the purposes of a particular law reform project.

In a few jurisdictions, a practice has emerged of law reform being regarded as the responsibility of the main legal interests, such as the law society, the bar and the law schools of the universities. One or several of these interests may form a committee, rather than establish an institute, to consider law reform issues and report from time to time.

2.3 Legislation and law reform

The law reform process results in recommendations that the law be changed, which normally requires legislation.

The product of a law reform process is a recommendation that the law be changed. For law reform to be complete, that recommendation must be implemented, nearly always, by legislation. In most, if not all, common law jurisdictions, the legislative agenda is largely set by the government. So, for law reform recommendations to be enacted, they must be accepted (in whole or in part) by the government. Where a law reform agency is established by statute, the scheme of the Act will usually require the law reform agency's recommendations to be directed to the government.

This will usually mean that, even once they are accepted by the government, the legislative recommendations made by a law reform agency have to compete for time in the legislature with the government's own proposed legislation. One way round this, adopted in a small number of jurisdictions to date, is for the law reform agency's recommendations to be subject to a special legislative procedure. The challenges of implementation are dealt with in Chapter 8.

How does law reform fit into the scheme of government legislation as a whole? A government's legislative policy will derive from a number of sources including the governing party's manifesto at the last election, policy developed by partisan think-tanks or outside interests aligned with the governing party, the policy priorities of ministries, pressure from back-bench members of the legislature and the need to react to events. From the government's perspective, the law reform agency is just one of those potential sources of legislation.

All governments have systems for delivering a programme of legislation. There is a wide range of these systems, and they vary significantly in time frame, the autonomy they allow to departments and the associated decision-making process. One feature that is largely common, however, is that there are often more potential bills than legislative slots.

In all parliamentary democracies, the amount of legislative time available to the government will be limited. As a result, the government has to prioritise its legislative programme, and its main policy concerns will take priority in the competition for scarce legislative slots. Law reform proposals may have a lower

Making a legislative programme in the United Kingdom Parliament

The creation of the United Kingdom Government's legislative programme, contained in the Queen's Speech on the opening of each parliamentary session, is short term and centrally controlled.

At the centre is a Cabinet committee, currently denominated Parliamentary Business and Legislation (PBL). It is chaired by a member of the Cabinet, usually the Leader of the House. About a year before the Queen's Speech, PBL asks departments to submit legislative bids in order of priority. The policy behind each bid has to be separately approved at Cabinet level. The number of bills to go into parliament varies, but is usually about 25 to 30. PBL usually receives twice that many bids. Bids are assessed on political importance, urgency and practical readiness. A provisional programme is agreed, and PBL monitors the development of the proposed bills by departments. PBL also authorises the use of Parliamentary Counsel to draft the legislation. The decision on the final content of the programme is made by Cabinet about a month before the Queen's Speech.

To reach parliament, a relevant report by the Law Commission for England and Wales or the Scottish Law Commission must first be accepted by the department with lead responsibility and receive Cabinet policy clearance. The department must then decide to include it in its bid to PBL and for it to feature not too far down the department's list. It must then be provisionally accepted by PBL, and receive drafting authorisation, which is needed regardless of whether the report had a draft bill attached. Finally, it must be included in the final list as decided by Cabinet.

priority. Indeed, it will not usually be the law reform agency that is directly involved in promoting the legislation, but rather the government department within whose remit the relevant area of law falls, and which has accepted the recommendations.

As a result, law reform agencies may frequently find it a challenge to ensure that their accepted recommendations are included in the government's legislative agenda. While most law reform agencies succeed some or most of the time in the implementation of their recommendations by government legislation, law reform agency bills commonly represent only a relatively small part of the legislature's workload.

2.4 Law reform agencies: key features and core values

Law reform agencies bring expertise, focus, continuity and independence to the task of law reform.

Law reform agencies offer a number of advantages for generating law reform proposals.

2.4.1 Expertise

Law reform agencies build up expertise, knowledge and specialist contacts in both the law and law reform. This is vital for successful law reform. It increases the likelihood of consistently high-quality work. A law reform agency's reputation and independence is also important in attracting skilled commissioners, staff and consultants.

Apart from its own collective expertise, a law reform agency can obtain additional expertise and advice from a wide range of stakeholders, cultivating dynamic relationships. For example, it can seek to capture the attention of external persons through open, thorough, imaginative and responsive consultations. As a result, opinions can not only be obtained from all quarters but are also taken fully and seriously into account. Consultation is more fully dealt with in Chapter 6. Some agencies also use consultants, who are mainly legal experts who assist with aspects of particular projects. Law reform agencies often also appoint working parties of experts, representatives from non-governmental organisations and other interested parties.

A law reform agency's methods ensure that its recommendations are thoroughly worked through before they reach the government and legislature. Its publications, and especially its final reports, are authoritative documents. They provide detailed and up-to-date explanations of the current law and of its deficiencies (both in principle and in practice), as well as recommendations for its improvement.

2.4.2 Focus

A law reform agency has the great advantage of having a central focus and purpose: law reform. As Lord Gardiner, the Lord Chancellor of England and Wales, said when introducing the bill to establish the original British law commissions, 'it may be your Lordships' experience that things in life do not get done unless it is somebody's job to do them. It has never been anybody's job in England … to see that our law is in good working order and kept up-to-date.'

As a result, a law reform agency can concentrate its energy and resources on this single purpose and is saved from the need to prioritise other work, as may be the case in other bodies, and most particularly government ministries.

2.4.3 Continuity

Law reform agencies are standing bodies. There are enormous advantages to having law reform undertaken by a body that is in continual existence. Continuity enables an agency to acquire and apply its expertise in the long term, avoiding the need for transient bodies each having to learn the necessary skills and processes. In many jurisdictions, law reform commissioners and staff may tend to stay longer within a law reform agency than government ministers and officials, building up a corporate memory of sound law reform methodology.

Law reform agencies usually undertake work in many areas of law, providing a standing body capable of producing recommendations in a range of legal areas, including substantive, evidential and procedural law. As a standing body, a law reform agency is able to discuss with government, over a number of years if necessary, the reasons for its recommendations, and their strengths and any weaknesses.

As a standing body, a law reform agency is readily available to take on more urgent law reform work, sometimes at short notice.

Another advantage of a standing law reform agency comes from the skills it acquires over time. One way in which they are accumulated is through the experience it gains from successive law reform projects. When a law reform agency has completed a law reform project, it can assess its performance during the project. The main benefit is to share within the agency what have been the successful, and less successful, methods used. The purpose is to learn from experience and therefore to confirm their processes and to improve them where necessary.

An entirely different type of evaluation can be used to assess the outcome of a completed law reform report that has already been implemented. Such an evaluation can be undertaken by the agency, the government or, probably best, both together. For example, the Ugandan Law Reform Commission has on occasion made post-enactment evaluations of some of 'their' legislation.

2.4.4 Independence

An essential feature, and a key advantage, of a law reform agency is its independence. It is not only independent of government in the conclusions it comes to in undertaking law reform, but also independent of judges, the legal professions and funders. This independence is critical to demonstrating that the views of a law reform agency are the result of rational enquiry based on meticulous research and consultation. The executive and the legislature frequently need and value specialist advice in the planning and formulation of law reform.

New Zealand and Malawi: Embedded independence

The Law Commission Act 1985, which established the New Zealand Law Commission, provides in section 5 that the Law Commission 'must act independently in performing its statutory functions and duties, and exercising its statutory powers'. The Commission also has the power under section 6 of the Act 'to initiate proposals for the review, reform or development of any aspect of the law of New Zealand'.

The Malawi Constitution, in section 136, provides for the independence of the Malawi Law Commission: 'the Law Commission shall exercise its functions and powers independent of the direction or interference of any other person or authority.' The Law Commission Act of Malawi also refers to the 'independence and impartiality of the Commission' in section 14, in a proviso in relation to donations that it may receive. This ensures that contributions of resources whether financial or otherwise do not bring the Commission under the control, direction or authority of the donor or contributor.

England and Wales: A selection criterion

The Law Commission for England and Wales have used law reform project selection criteria in preparing for their Programmes of Law Reform that included the following criterion:

Suitability: whether or not the independent, non-political Commission is the most suitable to conduct the project.

This advice is best provided by an objective, impartial and independent body.

Independence, together with the practice of wide public consultation, enhances the credibility of a law reform agency's work, including with opposition members of the legislature.

Key ways in which governments can promote the independence of law reform agencies include ensuring that appointments of commissioners are non-political and free from conflicts of interest, that the terms of reference for law reform projects are not designed to produce any particular outcome, and that there is no improper governmental or other external pressure upon the agency to produce any particular recommendations.

Often, it will be the government that asks the law reform agency to investigate a particular topic. The government may also exercise a veto over consideration of a topic by the agency. However, what is critical is that the agency is independent in how it comes to its own law reform conclusions. The Kenya Law Reform Commission sums this up well:

> *[Independence] refers to a Commission's intellectual independence – the willingness to make findings and offer non-partisan advice and recommendations to government without fear or favour.*

The establishment of agencies as independent by statute acts is a safeguard against interference by the government or any other body. Few enabling statutes refer specifically to 'independence'. There is the occasional exception, however.

However, as a public agency, a law reform agency must nonetheless remain accountable, for example by complying with public sector requirements on the use of funds and resources. The agency must also operate within boundaries established by its enabling statute. This may include agreeing on programmes of work with government and making annual reports to ministers to be laid before parliament. These are normal checks and balances applying to public agencies of all types. This does not constrain the law reform agency in exercising their law reform functions independently.

There are significant benefits in establishing a law reform agency with an independent status. If the agency is separate from the political process and political influence, and seen to be separate, it is regarded as objective and impartial. It thereby gains the trust and respect of the government and the legislature, as well as of stakeholders and of civic society generally. This enhances the credibility of the agency's recommendations.

This is valuable not only to the law reform agency, but also to the government and the legislature who need specialist advice in the formulation of law reform.

To safeguard the role of the law reform agency, some agencies take steps to ensure that their programme of work covers areas

Kenya: Key features and core values

The Kenya Law Reform Commission identifies the key features of a law reform agency as:

- independence
- expertise
- a focus on law reform
- continuity.

The Commission identifies the following as its core values:

- professionalism
- integrity
- innovation
- networking
- accountability
- results orientated.

The Commission also identifies the following as distinguishing characteristics:

- permanent
- authoritative
- full-time
- independent
- generalised
- consultative
- implementation-minded.

of policy and law appropriate for such an independent, non-political agency. An agency may apply selection criteria designed to safeguard that role.

Some law reform agencies have taken the step of expressly setting out their key features and core values in published documents.

2.5 The role of government

Regardless of how a law reform agency is constituted, to be effective in its functions the agency will have, or need to develop, channels of communication with the government. The agency will need to find ways of working with the government on matters such as the planning of law reform work, arranging for government consideration of reports and working towards the implementation of recommendations.

The statute or the agreement establishing a law reform agency may set out the working relationship with the government, as well as the agency's structure.

Where the law reform agency is a standard model independent statutory body, the founding legislation will generally make provision on the main aspects of the relationship between the agency and the government. The statute will therefore provide for the appointment of commissioners and the period of their tenure, their qualifications, and their remuneration and pensions. Usually, the Act will also provide for the staffing and funding of the agency.

Provision would also be made for the submission of reports by the agency to government or to ministers, for the agency to make programmes of work, subject to ministerial approval, and for the laying down by ministers before the legislature of agency programmes, reports and annual reports.

Where the law reform agency is an institute, the agreement establishing it may make provision for the submission of reports to the government, for requests from government to carry out a project to review a particular area of the law and for the institute to be able to seek funding for projects from other parties, including the government.

2.5.1 Guidance

The government and the law reform agency may issue guidance on the working relationships and the processes between the law reform agency and the government.

New Zealand: Cabinet Manual and Circular

In New Zealand, the Cabinet Manual, which has been endorsed by successive governments, provides authoritative guidance for ministers and their offices, and all government officials. The manual and Cabinet Office Circular issued in 2009, entitled 'Law Commission: Processes for Setting the Work Programme and Government Response to Reports', cover the processes for setting the Commission's work programme and for handling within the New Zealand Government, including consideration by the Cabinet of all Commission reports and recommendations. The circular provides that when a project is put on the Commission's work programme, government departments should make resources available to work on the project so that officials are kept in touch with the development of the project and can provide advice on it. The provision of legislative drafting assistance may also be appropriate so that a draft bill can be included in the Commission's report.

2.5.2 Protocols

A law reform agency may enter into a protocol or agreement with ministers or the government as to how they should work together in relation to law reform and law reform projects. Protocols may be made on the basis of statutory powers, or be entered into between the parties as an administrative measure.

Where such a protocol is made, it may contain provision on matters such as the following:

- the scope of the arrangement;

- designating formal contact points for the purposes of the protocol, on the part of both the law reform agency and the government;

- any requirements to be fulfilled before the law reform agency commences a project;

- matters on which agreement should be reached before the set-up of a project and during a project, for example the terms of reference;

- review points at which to consider progress;

- the overall timescale and a programme of regular communication about the project;

- the preparation of an impact assessment and government assistance in doing so, and any issues as to the powers of the legislature to legislate on the matter;

- arrangements after the project has been delivered, for example as to an interim response by ministers within a certain timescale, and for a full response, within a specified timescale, setting out ministers' views on accepting, rejecting or partially accepting individual recommendations;

- whether the commission is given the opportunity to discuss any significant recommendations to be either rejected or substantially modified; and

- any support to be given by the law reform agency to the government to assist implementation.

England and Wales: Protocols with two governments

As a result of devolution, England and Wales, while a single legal jurisdiction, has two legislatures, the United Kingdom Parliament and the National Assembly for Wales. At the executive level, the Welsh Government is responsible for devolved matters within Wales.

A protocol between the Lord Chancellor (on behalf of the United Kingdom Government) and the Law Commission for England and Wales was made in 2010, with statutory provision having been made for the protocol in section 3B(4) of the Law Commissions Act 1965 as a result of amendments made by the Law Commission Act 2009. A similar protocol was subsequently entered into between Welsh ministers and the Law Commission for England and Wales in 2015, the 1965 Act having been amended again to make such provision by the Wales Act 2014, in order to take account of Welsh devolution. The protocols cover the matters specified above.

2.6 Funding of law reform agencies

The funding of law reform agencies broadly follows the basis upon which the agency was established. The Act establishing a standard form agency will usually set out how it is to be funded. Funding, accordingly, is usually from the government budget, as approved by the legislature. However, there are a number of law reform agencies that receive a substantial proportion of their funding from donor agencies. This is particularly the case in developing countries and for individual specific projects.

Varieties of funding: Governments and donors

The Law Commission for England and Wales is entirely funded by the United Kingdom Government and other governmental entities. A mixture of core funding is provided by the Commission's sponsor ministry, the Ministry of Justice, as well as additional funds from other government departments, the Welsh Government and other public bodies in respect of specific law reform projects. In recent years, specific project funding has become more important.

The Scottish Law Commission, on the other hand, is wholly funded by the Scottish Government by way of core funding only.

The South African Law Reform Commission is funded by the South African Government. However, this commission has on occasion made use of donor funding for specific investigations. For instance, a German Government development agency (Deutsche Gesellschaft für Technische Zusammenarbeit) provided technical and financial assistance to enable the South African Law Reform Commission to acquire quantitative data and other information in relation to a project on the feasibility of establishing a compensation fund for victims of crime in South Africa.[7]

Where the law reform agency is an institute, funding is usually sought from entities such as ministries of justice, universities, law foundations and law societies.

Where the law reform function lies with a unit or department of government, that function is funded by the responsible ministry, as in Jamaica where the Legal Reform Department is managed centrally by the Ministry of Justice.

Alberta: The institute model

The Alberta Law Reform Institute is funded primarily by the Department of Justice and the Alberta Law Foundation. The University of Alberta provides office premises and other services, plus a small cash grant per annum.

2.7 The structure of law reform agencies

This section sets out the features of the standard model and the institute model for law reform agencies. It should be remembered that there are significant variations within each model, so not all existing law reform agencies will exhibit all of the features of one or other of the models.

2.7.1 The standard model

Most law reform agencies in Commonwealth countries exemplify the standard model. In this model, the key elements are that the agency:

- is a statutory body, having been established by legislation;

- has law reform as its only or main function;

- is a standing, permanent body;

- is independent of government and of other interests, such as the courts and the legal and other professions: their independence lies primarily in their intellectual independence, as regards their consideration of issues and making recommendations for law reform;

- receives all, or most, of its funding from government; some may also receive funding from donor agencies;

- usually has several commissioners, being persons appointed from different parts of the legal profession; occasionally, an agency has a small number of commissioners appointed from outside the legal profession;

- has as the norm a minimum of one full-time commissioner and/or a chief executive or similar post, except for law reform agencies in very small jurisdictions;

- has agreed programmes of work in the form of a programme or programmes of law reform, comprising a number of individual law reform projects on particular legal issues or topics;

- uses a broadly similar law reform methodology, including high-quality legal and other research; widespread consultation, drawing on outside expert assistance, such as from consultants, legal or otherwise, on the areas in question; and undertakes appropriate comparative work to consider the law in other jurisdictions;

- produces at the end of each project a final report, which is submitted to ministers or to government, and which examines the issues, and makes recommendations for reform, with full reasons for the changes proposed; and

- has its final report published – which is often accompanied by draft legislation that would implement the recommendations.

Most Commonwealth law reform agencies are 'classic' or standard model law reform agencies, established by statute. An alternative is the institute model, established by agreement between legal interests and stakeholders. The institute model is found at the state or provincial level in parts of Australia and Canada.

As stated above, there are variations in the model. For example, in some small jurisdictions, a commissioner may also be a member of the government. Many law reform agencies do not have in-house legislative drafting resources. In some standard model law reform commissions, not all commissioners will necessarily be lawyers.

There are also numerous variations in how law reform projects are undertaken, many of which are explored later in this guide.

The United Kingdom Commissions: The original standard model

The standard model was created by legislation establishing the Law Commission for England and Wales and the Scottish Law Commission. Both were established as statutory, independent bodies by the Law Commissions Act 1965.

These Commissions are independent as regards their law reform functions. They are permanent bodies.

Their general purpose is to promote law reform, with specific functions of keeping the law under review with a view to its systematic development and reform, including in particular the codification of such law, the elimination of anomalies, the repeal of obsolete and unnecessary enactments, the reduction of the number of separate enactments, and generally the simplification and modernisation of the law.

Provision is made for the appointment of commissioners. Commissioners in England and Wales (a chair and four other commissioners) are appointed by the Lord Chancellor. Following amendment as a consequence of devolution, commissioners in Scotland (a chair and up to four other commissioners) are appointed by Scottish ministers. Commissioners are usually appointed for a term not exceeding five years, although a limited renewal of appointment may be possible in certain circumstances. Commissioners' salaries are stipulated to be paid out of money provided by the United Kingdom Parliament and by Scottish ministers, respectively.

The statutory criteria for appointment are specified: those appearing to be suitably qualified by the holding of judicial office or by experience as an advocate or barrister or solicitor or equivalent, or as a teacher of law in a university. Those appointed as commissioners are usually experts in a particular area or areas of the law included in the Commission's current programme of law reform projects. A commissioner's role under this model is as a law reformer, leading and carrying out the law reform work, and undertaking peer review of other commissioners' work.

Provision is made for the preparation of programmes for the examination of different branches of the law with a view to reform; for the preparation of programmes of consolidation and statute law revision; for preparing draft bills; for providing advice and information to government and authorities; for the laying before the United Kingdom Parliament and the Scottish Parliament any programmes and proposals for reform; and for the making of an annual report to ministers, to be laid before the United Kingdom Parliament or the Scottish Parliament. Each programme lasts for a specified numbers of years and comprises a number of individual law reform projects of varying size.

New Zealand Law Commission: Commissioners can be drawn from other disciplines

In New Zealand law, the Law Commission Act 1985 does not require that all commissioners are legally qualified. Section 9 requires that the president of the Commission must be either a judge or a retired judge of the Court of Appeal or the High Court, or must be an experienced barrister or solicitor, but the Act is silent on the qualifications of other commissioners. On occasion, commissioners have been appointed who have not been legally qualified because they have had other relevant qualifications and experience.

2.7.2 The institute model

The other main model for an independent law reform agency is that based on an agreement made between leading stakeholders or interests in the legal community, such as the attorney-general, the law society, university law schools and the bar association. There are currently a small number of institute model agencies at state and province level, all in Australia and Canada. They are broadly similar, but there are also several differences between them, for example some of their working practices and their funding sources differ, as well as their legal structures.

The institute model will usually have similar aims to a standard statute-based law reform agency. These may include reviewing the law with a view to modernisation; the elimination of defects; the simplification and consolidation of laws; the repeal of laws that are obsolete or unnecessary; and, in appropriate cases, the achievement of uniformity in the laws of federal sub-state units, and uniformity between those units and the federal level.

An institute may have a board, with members comprising representatives of the founding parties, such as the judiciary, the bar association, the law society, the attorney-general, universities and other members representing the community. The institute model board, unlike the standard model commission, usually comprises representatives or *ex officio* office-holders, rather than commissioners engaged full- or part-time in law reform. Institute boards are usually larger than commissions.

As in the standard model, however, the institute undertakes widespread consultation with key stakeholders and with the community, and the responses received inform the recommendations made in their report.

Similarly, final reports are submitted to government to consider for implementation. Reports, along with research papers and consultation papers, will usually be published by the institute in paper form and/or on their website. As with the standard model, practice varies as to whether legislative drafting is undertaken.

The first law reform 'institute' was developed by the Canadian province of Alberta in 1967: the Alberta Law Reform Institute was established only two years after the template for the standard model was set by the establishment of the United Kingdom law commissions. The Alberta model has been adapted in Australia and Canada to suit the circumstances in individual states and provinces. These law reform bodies are sometimes described as following the 'institute model', although it should be recognised that there are substantial differences between agencies within this very broad category.

The Alberta Law Reform Institute was created by agreement between the Province of Alberta, the Law Society of Alberta and the University of Alberta. The aim was to establish a full-time independent agency dedicated to maintaining, modernising and monitoring the law of Alberta.

The Alberta Law Reform Institute: Objectives and methodology

The objectives of the Alberta Law Reform Institute are:

1. The consideration of matters of law reform with a view to proposing to the appropriate authority the means by which law of Alberta may be made more useful and effective; and

2. The preparation of proposals for law reform in Alberta, with respect to both the substantive law and the administration of justice.

The Institute's law reform methodology is as follows:

- Suggestions for potential law reform projects come from many sources, including government, the public and the legal profession.

- Following a review process, and a decision to take on a project, legal counsel carry out research and analysis of the issues. They collaborate with the board and with an advisory committee of experts in preparing a consultation document that seeks views on the policy choices for reform.

- Following public consultation, the board and the advisory committee develop final policy recommendations for publication in a final report.

- A key role of a final report is to convince government of the need for law reform so that the recommendations will be implemented by legislation.

- Draft legislation to implement recommendations is attached to the final reports.

British Columbia Law Institute: Purposes

The broad purposes of the Institute, described in Article 2 of its constitution, are to:

- promote the clarification and simplification of the law and its adaptation to modern social needs;
- promote improvement of the administration of justice and respect for the rule of law; and
- promote and carry out scholarly legal research.

The Institute's operational approach is described in Chapters 6 and 7.

The Institute has a governance board of 14 members, representing the founding parties and the broader legal community. The board appoints a director as the head of the organisation, which has a small team of legal and administrative staff. The Institute is funded primarily by the Department of Justice and the Alberta Law Foundation. The University of Alberta provides office premises and other services, plus a small cash grant per annum.

A key feature of the institute model is that it is not, ordinarily, dependent on a government for its establishment. In British Columbia, a standard model commission existed from 1969 to 1997. When it was decided that funding for the commission would be withdrawn, the British Columbia Law Institute was established by its founder members as a society under provincial legislation. The Institute is funded by a combination of operational funding from the Law Foundation of British Columbia and the provincial government, and funding received from government programmes, not-for-profit grants and stakeholders for specific projects.

The institute model has spread successfully within both Canada and Australia, at the provincial and state level. The Tasmania Law Reform Institute was established in 2001 by agreement between the Government, the University and the Law Society of Tasmania, drawing on the model of the Alberta Law Reform Institute.

This model has also been adopted for both the Australian Capital Territory and, most recently, South Australia. That institute is based at Adelaide Law School and arose, in 2010, from an agreement between the Attorney-General of South Australia, the University of Adelaide and the Law Society of South Australia.

Notes

1   http://www.ulrc.go.ug/content/law-revision-department
2   http://revisedacts.lawreform.ie/revacts/intro
3   http://salawreform.justice.gov.za/anr/2015-2016-anr-salrc.pdf
4   For a discussion of 'common law codification' by the Law Commission for England and Wales, see http://www.lawcom.gov.uk/wp-content/uploads/2015/07/cp223_for_accessibility_wales_with_cover.pdf, pages 142–152.
5   Formally, simply 'the Law Commission'. It is referred to throughout this guide as 'the Law Commission for England and Wales' to avoid misunderstanding.
6   David Easton, 'An Approach to the Analysis of Political Systems' (1956–7) 9 World Politics 383; Robert H Jackson, *The Supreme Court in the American System of Government* (Cambridge Mass, Harvard University Press, 1955).
7   http://salawreform.justice.gov.za/reports/r_prj82-2011-victim-compensation.pdf

Chapter 3

The Initiation of Law Reform Projects

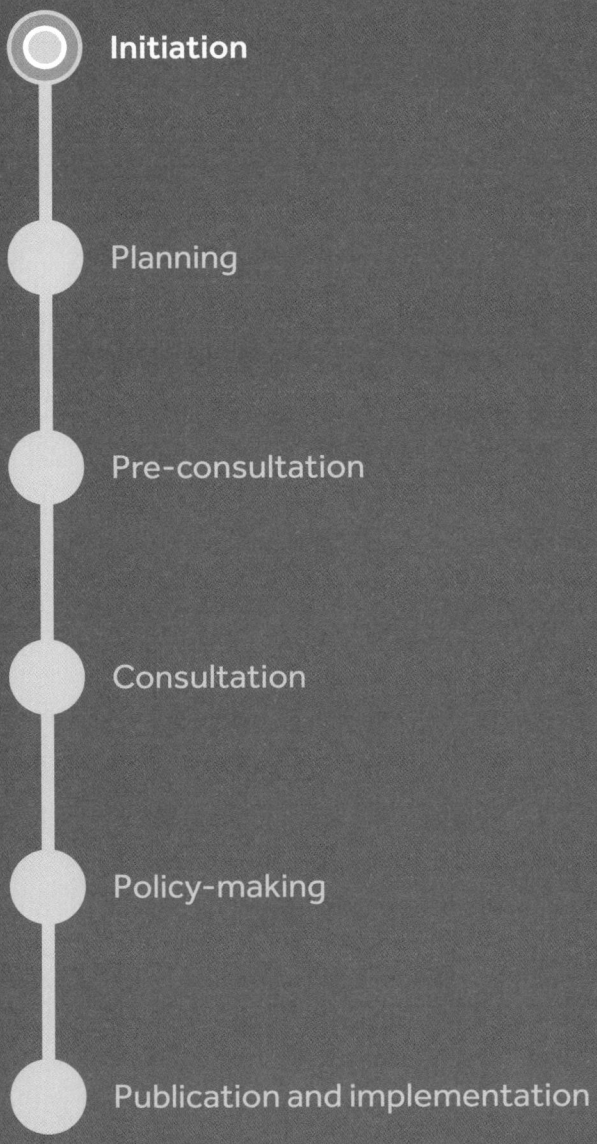

Initiation

Planning

Pre-consultation

Consultation

Policy-making

Publication and implementation

Chapter 3
The Initiation of Law Reform Projects

Chapter 3 looks at how law reform projects are initiated. The starting point is the mandate – statutory or otherwise – of the agency, which is usually very broad. It then looks at how an agency can select types of project, and discusses the advantages and disadvantages of each. Under the theme of relations with government, it looks at the ways in which a law reform agency receives or decides upon work, whether in references from government or in programmes of work generated by the agency itself (albeit usually approved by governments). The chapter also looks at the institutionalisation of relations with governments as an integral part of the process. The selection criteria for law reform projects are then considered. Finally, the chapter looks at how law reform fits the contemporary context, as well as some of the current challenges to law reform.

This chapter deals with how law reform agencies initiate or select individual law reform projects. It does so by considering five related elements: the scope of the agency's mandate, its relationship with other agencies, the process it uses for selecting projects and the criteria used, as well as the contemporary context within which selection is made.

Most law reform agency mandates are extremely wide in scope, and this presents the first selection challenge: how to use limited resources to best effect. This challenge can be greatly assisted where the agency has good working relationships with other law reform agencies and comparable bodies, both domestically and internationally. Selection outcomes are also strengthened where the process for selection is well structured and consultative, involving assistance from other law reform partners such as government ministries, legal professionals and non-governmental organisations. The selection criteria should allow the agency to identify which projects best match its core skills and resources.

The context within which projects are selected is significant: at different times, specific areas of law may require examination, or the general financial or political setting may suggest the need for prioritising certain areas for review. Contemporary topics include the regulation of information and communications technology.

3.1 The scope of the law reform agency's mandate

Most law reform agency mandates are wide. Selection and prioritisation of projects are inevitable. Often, it will be advisable for a law reform agency's programme to include a mixture of narrow-focus, short-duration projects and wider focus, longer term, more expansive projects.

The wide scope of most law reform agencies' mandates significantly influences the actual content of a work programme. As discussed in Chapter 2, generally, law reform agencies are given a very wide-ranging mandate: to keep the *entire law* of their jurisdiction under review and to make proposals for reform of that law. Statutes also frequently task agencies with codifying and consolidating all of that law.

At first sight, this may suggest that the agency is required to reform *all of the law* of its jurisdiction, and perhaps to codify, or consolidate, all of it. This may have been the founders' original intention, but it can never have been understood to preclude prioritisation. The reality is that selection is inevitable and is conditioned by the context in which the agency finds itself.

Most law reform agencies are public bodies, and are either entirely state funded, sometimes with contributions from donor agencies, or funded through an institution such as a university. The result is that most law reform agencies have relatively modest resources. This may be especially the case for an agency in a small state or territory.

The budget, like that of most public bodies, will also be subject to regular, usually annual, oversight, in keeping with national and international public service governance obligations or 'value for money' requirements. A law reform agency will usually find it necessary to justify its budget with regard to its outputs. For many, this will involve an expectation of measurable outputs in each year.

Law reform agencies usually develop their programmes by selecting a variety of projects from the spectrum available, from narrowly focused law reform projects that aim to solve small-scale and clearly identified problems, to large-scale projects, or series of projects, that aim to reform or codify major areas of the substantive or adjectival law of the jurisdiction. Such programmes must also take into account other functions such as consolidation and revision and the repeal of obsolete statutes.

Often, it will be advisable for a law reform agency, in establishing its programme, to include a mixture of narrow-focus, short-duration projects, and wider focus, longer term, more expansive, substantive law reform projects.

3.1.1 Selecting narrow-focus projects

Where clear difficulties have been identified in the application of the law by government, by an inquiry looking into wider issues, or by stakeholders and academics, it may be possible for a law reform agency to undertake a relatively short, substantive law reform project to quickly identify solutions.

Narrow-focus projects on missing persons in Scotland and Ireland; Criminal justice in South Africa

Two projects on the civil law relating to missing persons:

- The Scottish Law Commission's *Report on Presumption of Death*[1] recommended legislation that would permit both the registration of death and the issuing of a death certificate in respect of a missing person who may be presumed dead. Previously, Scottish law had allowed for a presumption of death in only limited circumstances. The Commission's report was implemented in the Presumption of Death (Scotland) Act 1977.

- The Law Reform Commission of Ireland's *Report: Civil Law Aspects of Missing Persons*[2] examined the civil law issues that arose when a person goes missing, such as the need to manage their property on an interim basis, whether it should be presumed that the missing person is alive or has died, and the civil status of the missing person and of those left behind (notably, their married or civil partnership status).

Two projects in South Africa on criminal justice:

- The South African Law Reform Commission's report on the expungement of certain criminal records reviewed the different systems used for the keeping of criminal records and their expungement in South Africa, at the request of the Minister of Justice and Constitutional Development. The Commission focused on compliance with constitutional imperatives, the prescribed process and the qualifying criteria for expungements.[3]

- The South African Law Reform Commission considered reform of the system of trapping – known as entrapment in other jurisdictions – in light of the impact of human rights norms and trends in other parts of the world. The Commission's recommendations that there should be greater judicial control over trapping, with the courts being given a broader discretion, led to the adoption of Criminal Procedure Second Amendment Act 85 of 1996.[4]

In addition, where an agency has responsibility for consolidation or statute revision, a small consolidation or revision bill could be prepared.

3.1.2 Selecting wide-ranging projects

The wide scope of most mandates inevitably, and correctly, leads to an expectation that the law reform agency should select and complete not only narrow-focus projects, but also wide-ranging projects to codify large areas of law. Sometimes, such projects will be expected as a contribution by the law reform agency to broader institutional or political projects.

East African Community: Commercial law co-ordination

The East African Community Partner States are Burundi, Kenya, Rwanda, Tanzania and Uganda. Article 126 of the East African Community Treaty provides that partner states shall, through their appropriate national institutions, take all necessary steps to harmonise all their national laws that relate to the East African Community. The East African Community established a sub-committee on the approximation of national laws, headed by the law reform agencies of the East African Community Partner States, to monitor the implementation of this objective. Among the areas being monitored by the sub-committee are contract law, immigration, insolvency, intellectual property, labour and employment, and the sale of goods.

More commonly, a law reform agency will perceive, or be convinced of, the need for wide-ranging change in both the form and the substance of a large area of law, often through codification.

While the Australian Law Reform Commission report (see 'Large-scale codification projects', opposite page) has been implemented, efforts to codify the criminal law in England and Wales and in Scotland have not, to date, succeeded in legislative reform.

Large-scale codification projects should not be taken on without careful consideration, given the significant resources required and the degree of complexity involved.

One possible conclusion from this is that caution should be exercised in selecting large-scale projects, in light of the significant resources required and the degree of complexity involved. For this reason, some law reform agencies have, at different times in their history, avoided such large projects on the grounds that it may not be efficient to spend limited resources on a project that can take a number of years to complete, and whose implementation may only be decided many years from the start date.

Nonetheless, there are a number of reasons why, in spite of the challenges identified, agencies sometimes continue to select large codification projects:

- There may be external reasons why large codification projects must be undertaken, including the requirements of membership of regional organisations.

- Codification may be particularly useful in developing countries that are undertaking transformational processes such as implementing a new constitutional or governance framework (see the example box below 'Constitutional development and implementation: Kenya').

- Codification may come back into favour in a state or territory where codification projects had, in the past, not been implemented; for example, in 2015 the

Large-scale codification projects

South Africa is one of the few countries worldwide that makes specific provision in its constitution for the protection of the rights of children. One of the major considerations in the South African Law Reform Commission's project reviewing the Child Care Act[5] was the meaningful expansion and support of this provision of the Bill of Rights. The investigation culminated in the comprehensive and ground-breaking Children's Act 38 of 2005, which consolidates and reforms the law on matters related to children, effectively creating a legislative code. It deals with topics including the age of majority, paternity, custody, child support, guardianship, parenting plans, children's courts, circumcision, day care, child protection, foster care, group homes, adoption, surrogacy, child abduction and the trafficking of children.

In two reports on insurance contracts, published in 1980 and 1982, the Australian Law Reform Commission recommended wholesale reform of the law relating to insurance contracts in Australia, which had become seriously outdated. The reports dealt with the law relating to insurance intermediaries – brokers and agents – and their relationship with insurers and the broader adequacy and appropriateness of the law of insurance contracts. At the time, the law in this area was a mixture of common law and Imperial, federal, and state statutes.[6] The reports continue to influence consideration by law reform agencies of reform of insurance contract law in other jurisdictions, including the United Kingdom and Ireland.

The work of the Law Commission for England and Wales (in the 1970s and 1980s) on codifying criminal law culminated in the report *A Criminal Code for England and Wales* in 1989,[7] which included a draft Criminal Code Bill. The bill, produced largely by a working group of academics attached to the Commission, sought to codify both the general part of the criminal law of England and Wales (conduct and mental elements, parties to offences, intoxication, etc.) and the main substantive offences. The Scottish Law Commission similarly published a draft Criminal Code for Scotland in 2003.[8]

Law Commission for England and Wales returned to codification in the criminal law area with a project that involves complete codification of procedural sentencing law.[9]

- It will be expected, because of the wide mandate of law reform agencies, that large codification projects should form part of the standard make-up of their work programme; that is, involving a balance of smaller and larger projects. This is notably the case in states and territories where codification has never been out of favour, and may be expected in those (relatively few) states where a law reform agency has been established in a jurisdiction with a civil law tradition (such as Rwanda).

If a large-scale project is undertaken, no doubt following especially careful consideration of the risks involved, it would merit particularly thorough planning.

Furthermore, while law reform agencies should pay attention to the extent to which their recommendations are implemented, this cannot, as discussed in Chapter 8, be the sole measure of success. Therefore, a completed codification project on an important area of law, such as criminal law, can serve as an authoritative, and thus invaluable, statement of the law. This may

A strategy for large-scale projects

In handling large-scale projects, the British Columbia Law Institute has found the following strategy beneficial:

- Start with a scoping research project (Phase 1). Use Phase 1 to determine the issues to be addressed and set out a plan for the larger project, perhaps narrowing the issues to keep the project manageable.

- When tackling the larger project, consider whether topics are discrete enough to be appropriate for interim reports on the topic or can be handled independently of the whole. It is not always appropriate to do this, but if it is possible, it ensures successes along the way, which is a positive outcome for staff, volunteers and stakeholders. The Institute has adopted this with their Strata Property Law project, which went into year 5, during which two reports were issued, the first of which has already been implemented during the course of the overall project.[10]

- Alternatively, the project can be broken up into a number of sub-projects (as with the Institute's project on wills, estates and succession) so that the reports can be worked on simultaneously.

be a significant consideration for a law reform agency operating in a small jurisdiction, where there may not be a commercial market for law publishers to support textbooks on the law of that jurisdiction.

3.1.3 Consolidation, revision and repeal

When developing a programme, a law reform agency will look to include projects expressing all of its active functions. Many law reform agencies have ongoing mandates in connection with the legislative stock of a state or territory, involving the maintenance and state of the statute book. This can include:

Some law reform agencies have an explicit mandate to maintain the statute book, including by preparing consolidation bills and repealing obsolete legislation.

- preparing consolidation bills;

- preparing bills repealing obsolete legislation;

- preparing selections of revised Acts, which are administrative consolidations (Acts-as-amended) that may not necessarily require parliamentary enactment, but may nonetheless have semi-official status; and

- preparing and maintaining the entire legislative stock, sometimes referred to as preparing and maintaining 'the Laws of' the state or territory.

As noted above, this type of mandate may require a law reform agency to select either specific areas of law to consolidate as part of its ongoing work programme or to engage in a complete compilation, or update of a previous compilation, of the statute law of the state or territory.

The selection of projects will therefore be affected by the extent to which a law reform agency's mandate includes such explicit responsibilities to maintain the statute book, as well as the importance attached to this aspect of its work. Such work is more likely to play an important role in a small state or territory where the agency may be the only realistic source of authoritative information on current legislation.

3.1.4 Wider mandates still

Even if a law reform agency's mandate includes a review of the entire law of the jurisdiction, as it typically will, there are some implied limits to the scope of its work. As discussed in Chapter 2, no law reform agency is likely to take on projects of an overtly partisan political nature.

A few law reform agencies have mandates to carry out other activities, such as undertaking educational programmes on relevant law.

Nonetheless, a small number of law reform agencies have been given a wider remit that includes an explicit obligation to engage in activities that might be regarded as closer to those carried out by a ministry as part of policy formation or by a body such as an economic or social research agency.

The Malawi Law Commission, for example, is expressly required by its foundation legislation to carry out civic education of the general public in connection with its law reform mandate. As a result of this, in a project aimed at determining whether or not the law on the use of contraceptives should be amended in order to address HIV/AIDS, that commission investigated the extent to which possible reforms would be consistent with, or conflict with, existing social practices, through engagement in community-based workshops.

Among its other functions, the Kenya Law Reform Commission is statutorily required to undertake public education on matters relating to law reform. The Victorian Law Reform Commission undertakes educational programmes on law reform relevant to their work.

Constitutional development and implementation: Kenya

The role of the Kenya Law Reform Commission in implementing Kenya's 2010 constitution is recognised in the text of this constitution. Working with the relevant government department, the Commission developed model laws (launched in November 2016) to operationalise the constitution's devolution of functions to newly created county governments.[11]

Even without such an explicit statutory provision, however, many law reform agencies have engaged in comparable qualitative, and sometimes empirical, exercises as part of law reform projects.

The Australian Law Reform Commission's research on aboriginal law involved a large number of community-based meetings with tribal elders to explore the position in practice in Australia in advance of making recommendations for reform.[12]

Another example, related to a more traditional law reform project, reform of the jury system, is the New Zealand Law Commission's empirical research on jury comprehension, in conjunction with university-based partners, which assisted the Commission's recommendations on how to improve juror comprehension.[13]

Similarly, the Law Reform Commission of Ireland, as part of a project on harmful digital communications, engaged the relevant Ministry for Children and Youth Affairs to facilitate workshops with young people in Ireland on the subject matter of that project in order to conduct a representative and qualitative assessment of their views on the legal regulation of harmful digital communications.[14]

3.2 Relations with other law reform agencies

Many law reform agencies are either required by their founding legislation, or may in any event choose, to engage in joint projects with other bodies, including other law reform agencies. This necessarily involves close liaison with law reform agencies and other bodies to ensure that the selection of the subject matter for such a joint project is suitable for each body involved. The impetus for such a joint project can arise from a number of factors.

One is the need for the harmonisation of laws within federal or legislatively devolved states.

There may also be a need for harmonisation in the context of a regional economic union, such as the major project on the harmonisation of commercial law in the East African Community (see example box above 'East African Community: commercial law co-ordination').

In addition, law reform agencies have developed formal and informal international links to facilitate the exchange of ideas, which may be useful in connection with the initiation of projects, as they will be for other aspects of agencies' work. The two formal associations are the Commonwealth Association

Law reform agencies share experiences and ideas in order to learn from each other and occasionally to harmonise laws. The Commonwealth Association of Law Reform Agencies (CALRAs) is one of the formal associations of law reform agencies.

Australia and the United Kingdom

In Australia, federal, state and territory law reform agencies sometimes engage, or liaise with each other, in projects with a view to producing a 'Uniform Act', in effect a harmonisation statute that can be enacted in each state or territory.

In the United Kingdom, the two Commissions, in England and Wales and Scotland, have a long tradition of undertaking joint projects. During the period in which the Northern Ireland Law Commission was active,[15] the Commissions also undertook two tripartite projects. Each of the Commissions is under a statutory duty to consult with the others.

Law reform agencies maintain linkages with other bodies involved in reform, such as human rights commissions.

of Law Reform Agencies and the Association of Law Reform Agencies of Eastern and Southern Africa (see Appendix 2). Links between the Australian, New Zealand and Pacific agencies benefit from the conferences organised from time to time under the banner of the Australasian Law Reform Agencies Conference. Similarly, there are annual meetings of the five law commissions of England and Wales, Scotland, Northern Ireland (when active), Jersey and the Republic of Ireland.

Bilateral links between law reform agencies have sometimes developed because of historic associations between two countries, rather than because of regional associations. An example is the link between the Malawi Law Commission and the Scottish Law Commission for co-operation and capacity-building for law reform. This was agreed as part of a wider project called Capacity Building for Justice, which began in 2010 and lasted for a period of three years. The project arose out of the Scotland–Malawi Governmental Agreement in 2005 for mutual co-operation and assistance, and so attracted government development funding for capacity-building activities. Such associations provide the potential for mutual co-operation and learning, including in the context of the selection of projects.

3.3 Relations with bodies with different remits

In many states and territories, bodies other than the law reform agency may have specific law reform mandates in particular legal areas. This can have the effect that law reform agencies may hesitate to conduct projects within those areas, even where that agency has a wide, 'all of the law' remit.

For example, a statutory regulatory body, such as an agency with responsibility for environmental protection or occupational safety and health, may be given responsibility for carrying out regular post-legislative statutory reviews of the legislation in question. Such post-legislative scrutiny may require the agency to prepare a report for the relevant government ministry as to whether or not the legislation is working effectively and whether or not some reforms are required. It is highly likely that a law reform agency will not select a project that would overlap with the specialist review role given to an agency in a specialised area of the law.

Similarly, in some jurisdictions, legislation may provide for a statutory post-legislative review of the legislation by a ministry. Again, such specific review requirements are likely to preclude a review by a law reform agency of these areas, although it may not preclude a ministry from 'contracting out' such a review to a law reform agency. Such reviews may indeed be shared between a ministry and a law reform agency (such as the review of New Zealand's Search and Surveillance Act 2012[16] where the statute itself provided for a joint review).

A state may be required, as part of its international obligations, to establish a national human rights agency, with responsibility to monitor the extent to which the state has implemented its international human rights obligations. This may include, for instance, advising as to whether proposed legislation is compatible with the relevant human rights norms.

While such a function can be conferred on a law reform agency, it is more common for a separate human rights agency to be established. In that case, those functions would in practice fall outside the scope of projects that the law reform agency will consider.

Nonetheless, a law reform agency is likely to engage in an examination of whether an area of current law should be reformed in order to comply with human rights standards, whether national or international. To that extent, a law reform agency may be involved in selecting a project that necessarily has a human rights dimension.

For example, a commonly selected criminal law project for a law reform agency is reform of the law on self-defence. This involves an examination of the extent to which lethal force may be used in self-defence, engaging the application of the right to life and issues such as the state's positive obligation to protect the right to life and the use of fatal force by agents of the state.

In any event, where both a law reform agency and a separate human rights agency have been established in a state, it is likely that both bodies will wish to establish close links having regard to their overlapping functions.

In summary, law reform projects often clearly involve a consideration of wide policy matters. An important issue for a law reform agency in selecting a project is therefore whether or not it has the capacity, alone or with another agency, to analyse and understand the wider policy context within which the legal reform issues must be assessed.

3.4 The selection process: programmes, references and other functions

Law reform agencies tend to undertake projects that are in a set programme containing a list of projects or are referred to them by government.

A key aspect in the selection process is whether a law reform agency operates through a programme, which contains a defined list of projects to be completed over a defined timescale, or on the basis of commissioned references from, for example, a justice minister or attorney-general. Although this appears, at first sight, to present a binary 'either/or' question, in practice the distinction between programme-based and commissioned references is often subtler. Many law reform agencies will initiate projects from both sources.

3.4.1 Programmes

Many law reform agencies are mandated, whether by their founding legislation or by non-statutory terms of reference, to prepare programmes of law reform. These programmes contain a defined list of projects to be completed over a specific time frame. It is also common that such a programme must be approved by a ministry or by the entire government/Cabinet.

While it is possible that a law reform agency might choose to select the projects for a programme of law reform on the basis of a purely internal selection process, dependent on decision-making by the commissioners or board members, this is unlikely to be the case in practice. Many law reform agencies will, either by legislative requirement or because of good governance practices, engage in a detailed consultative process in order to develop a draft list of projects for inclusion in a programme. This consultation will usually involve engagement with government ministries, other state agencies, legal professionals, other professions, non-governmental organisations and the public generally.

In recent years, online consultation and the use of social media has become an important feature of such consultative processes. Direct live meetings with interested parties also remain, however, an important component of consultation.

When a law reform agency engages with government ministries as part of the selection process, it is likely that this will provide a clear view of the priorities within key ministries, such as the justice ministry. This has the benefit of an appreciation of whether or not particular projects under consideration by the agency would be at least consistent with the ministry's general objectives at that time. In turn, this has the advantage that, if the agency selects such a project, it may therefore (when the project is completed) be considered favourably by the ministry when it puts forward its priorities in what is often a contest in a state or territory for limited parliamentary time.

In any event, as noted above, a law reform agency's foundation legislation or terms of reference will often provide that the law reform agency's draft programme of selected projects will require formal approval by either a specific minister or the entire government/Cabinet. Therefore, a well-conducted consultative process, which has included consideration of the views of ministries as well as the general public, is also more likely to be successful in obtaining such formal approval.

Programme construction: England and Wales

The statute establishing the Law Commission for England and Wales requires it 'to prepare and submit to the Minister [the Lord Chancellor] from time to time programmes for the examination of different branches of the law with a view to reform'. Currently, programmes typically last for three years and include projects proposed by a variety of actors. In the tenth programme (2008), for instance, a project on the law relating to social services support for adults was proposed by the parents of two adult disabled children, the Law Society and a mental health charity. The Commission's subsequent recommendations (2011) were enacted as the Care Act 2014 and the Social Services and Well-Being (Wales) Act 2014.

Government departments and public bodies other than the Ministry of Justice now routinely 'bid' for projects in the Law Commission's programme. The 11th programme (2011) included projects on data sharing among public bodies (proposed by the Cabinet Office), electronic communications (Department for Culture, Media and Sport), electoral law (the Electoral Commission, for a joint project with the other UK commissions), taxi and private hire vehicle regulation (Department for Transport), the tort of unjustified threats in relation to trade marks (the Intellectual Property Office) and wildlife law (Department for the Environment, Food and Rural Affairs). The departments involved made financial contributions to the Commission in relation to the projects they proposed.

3.4.2 References

Some law reform agencies operate either entirely, or else in part, on the basis of commissioned work from a minister or attorney-general. These might be referred to as 'references', 'referrals' or 'requests'.

For example, the (federal) Australian Law Reform Commission operates entirely on the basis of a rolling programme of work consisting of a series of commissioned projects from federal ministers.

Many other law reform agencies operate on the basis of a combination of programmes and occasional commissioned references. The balance between programme projects and references may vary over time and between agencies.

Such references, whether they are the only source of law reform projects or are combined with programmes, may be mandatory in the sense that the law reform agency must deal with a commissioned project: it has no choice to decline the project. However, it is common practice that, before the relevant minister or attorney-general makes a formal reference to the law reform agency, there will be informal discussion as to the precise form of the reference and the capacity of the agency to deal with it. In many jurisdictions, the statute may not clearly require a law reform agency to accept a reference. In the United Kingdom, the Law Commissions will, following initial discussions, decline a reference that is thought to be unsuitable. The statutory protocol between the United Kingdom Government and the Law Commission for England and Wales recognises the freedom of the Commission to decline a reference, and sets out the criteria for such a decision.

As the example above indicates, projects included in a programme may well nonetheless be proposed by government departments or other public bodies. In such circumstances, such projects are treated in the same way as projects proposed by others, and subject to the same process of consideration and selection. However, clearly one step that does not have to be taken in relation to such projects is determining the attitude of the relevant government agency to the proposal.

On the other hand, in some cases, the distinction between a programme item and a reference may not be very significant. For instance, in relation to the Law Commission for England and Wales's 11th Programme of Law Reform (see example box above, 'Programme construction: England and Wales'), a project on the regulation of healthcare professionals was proposed by the Department of Health as part of the consultation process, but accepted by the Commission as a reference before the programme was finalised.

3.4.3 Official inquiries

A further source of work for law reform agencies may be recommendations from independent commissions or other bodies set up to investigate particular issues. In most jurisdictions, such recommendations must still be either referred to the law reform agency by a minister or included in a programme.

Double jeopardy: An inquiry-initiated project

The racist murder of a young black man, Stephen Lawrence, in London in 1993 led in 1999 to a wide-ranging public inquiry chaired by Sir William Macpherson, a retired judge. One of its recommendations was that the Law Commission should consider the law on double jeopardy in England and Wales, the main suspects in the murder having been formally acquitted following a failed private prosecution. The Home Secretary immediately referred the question to the Law Commission, which reported in 2001, proposing a narrow exception to the rule. The government legislated a wider version of the proposals, which eventually led to the acquittal of one of the suspects being quashed in 2011. He was retried, with another defendant. Both were convicted and sentenced to life imprisonment.

3.4.4 Numbers and time frames

Whether a law reform agency operates primarily on the basis of a formal programme or primarily on the basis of commissioned projects, all law reform agencies will be engaged in a rolling programme of work.

Two connected questions arise concerning programmes:

- How many projects should be included in a law reform agency work programme (whether a formal programme of law reform or references or both)?

- What is the ideal time frame for a law reform agency work programme?

There is no simple answer to these questions. Both depend on the resources of the agency, the inherent size and complexity of

Sources for projects in selected law reform agencies

Law reform agency	Project sources		
	Programmes	References	Other
Alberta Law Reform Institute		X	X
Australian Law Reform Commission		X	
British Columbia Law Institute		X	X
Cayman Islands Law Reform Commission		X	X
Hong Kong, Law Reform Commission of		X	
Jersey Law Commission			X
Kenya Law Reform Commission	X	X	X
Law Commission for England and Wales	X	X	
Law Commission of India		X	X
Law Reform Commission of Nova Scotia		X	X
Law Commission of Ontario		X	X
Law Reform Commission of Ireland	X	X	
Law Reform Commission of Western Australia		X	
New South Wales Law Reform Commission		X	
New Zealand Law Commission	X	X	X
Northern Territory Law Reform Committee		X	
Queensland Law Reform Commission		X	
Scottish Law Commission	X	X	
South African Law Reform Commission	X	X	
South Australian Law Reform Institute		X	X
Tasmania Law Reform Institute		X	X
Victorian Law Reform Commission		X	X

the project, and outside pressures on timing from government or elsewhere.

In general, however, those law reform agencies that work on the basis of programmes of law reform generally operate on the basis of a life cycle of between three and five years. In some instances, the length of a programme may coincide with the term of office of a majority of the appointed commissioners or board members.

The longer the life cycle of a programme, the greater the number of specific projects that will be included in the programme. However, if the mixture between narrow-focus and wider projects favours more narrow-focus projects, then this will also affect the total number of projects included in a programme.

In any event, it has become common practice of many law reform agencies for projects from a previous programme to be carried over into, or overlap with, projects in a new programme. The annual reports of a commission-based law reform agency, such as the Australian Law Reform Commission, and a programme-based law reform agency, such as the Law Commission for England and Wales or the Scottish Law Commission, will therefore broadly resemble each other: they will both contain an analysis of projects under consideration, projects just begun, projects well under way, projects completed and projects implemented.

3.5 Selection criteria

Selection criteria are the general, high-level criteria or principles that many law reform agencies have developed in order to determine what type of law reform projects they should carry out. While there is a shared core to these criteria, the diverse form of law reform agencies means that there is no single transferable set of criteria.

Projects are selected according to the criteria of importance, suitability, and resource availability.

The core selection criteria for many law reform agencies, in the terms set out by the Law Commission for England and Wales, are:

- **importance**: the extent to which the law is unsatisfactory, and the potential benefits from reform;

- **suitability**: whether the independent non-political Commission is the most suitable body to conduct the review; and

- **resources**: the experience of commissioners and staff, the funding available, and whether the project meets the requirements of the programme.[17]

The Scottish Law Commission broadly follows the same approach to setting selection criteria; but sets out the national context, namely having regard to the Scottish Government's overall purpose for Scotland, the National Performance Framework and the national outcomes for Scotland. In addition, the Scottish Law Commission states that in selecting projects they bear in mind whether or not a bill on a project would be suitable for the special parliamentary processes, in particular for certain commission bills in the Scottish Parliament.[18]

Other approaches to selection: Victoria and South Africa

Victoria

The Victorian Law Reform Commission adopts a rather different approach to selection. It draws a distinction between references it receives from the Attorney-General of Victoria, on the one hand, and 'community law reform projects', on the other.

Community law reform projects address legal issues that are of general community concern, but are small enough to have relatively straightforward solutions. In addition, community law reform projects must not require significant resources.

In deciding whether to undertake a community law reform project, the Commission considers the following:[19]

- **The area in which the law applies:** the Commission can only make recommendations about state laws.

- **The scope of the community law reform project**: this includes the complexity of the legal issues raised, the amount of research required and the amount of legal change that may be needed. The Commission can only take on community law reform projects that deal with relatively small changes to the law.

- **The amount of community consultation that will be needed to fully consider the issue**: complex and controversial subjects or areas of law that do not have strong community consensus will generally not fit within community law reform projects. These types of issues require significant consultation and public debate to resolve. This is better suited to a government-initiated reference or inquiry.

- **The law reform proposal's likely public benefit**: the Commission is interested in projects that will fix problems with the law that affect a significant proportion of the population or address problems faced by significantly disadvantaged members of the community.

- **Community involvement**: if a community group is interested in putting forward a law reform idea, the Commission seeks to know how the group have consulted with people to check that the proposal meets their needs. The Commission also likes to know how the group proposing the idea will keep people informed and involved if the law reform idea is accepted as a community law reform project by the Commission.

- **The prospects of success for the reform proposal**: community law reform projects must provide a simple, effective solution to an anomaly, inequity or gap in the law.

- **The resources and time needed to undertake the community law reform project**: the legislation governing the Commission requires that community law reform projects must not require significant resources. The Commission prefers community law reform projects that can be completed within 12 months, using existing resources.

- **Avoiding duplication**: if the law has recently been considered by parliament or is currently being reviewed, or likely to be reviewed by government, the Commission will not undertake the project. If the law reform idea better suits consideration by another law reform organisation, the Commission will inform the person or organisation of who to approach.

Other approaches to selection: Victoria and South Africa (cont.)

South Africa

All requests received by the South African Law Reform Commission are assessed with reference to the Commission's selection criteria.[20] The criteria provide for a two-phased process to determine whether an investigation should be recommended for inclusion in the Commission's research programme. The first phase is an initial screening process to determine whether a proposal or request falls within the mandate of the Commission. The following aspects are addressed during this process:

- whether the issues concerned are predominantly legal;
- whether the legal problem can be addressed in a way that does not require a change of the law;
- whether there is another institution or government department better placed to deal with the request; and
- whether there are any pending legal developments that could influence the relevance of the investigation.

If all the above criteria are met, the request proceeds past the first phase and a preliminary investigation is undertaken during the second phase. Phase 2 is aimed at the evaluation of the request in greater depth to assist the Commission with advising the Minister of Justice and Constitutional Development on whether an investigation should be included in the Commission's research programme. Such a preliminary investigation must be concluded within a specified period and must be communicated to the requester. The criteria used in Phase 2 are the following:

- the extent to which the law may require reform;
- the scale of the problem in terms of the proportion of the community affected;
- the potential benefits likely to accrue from undertaking reform or repeal of the law;
- the extent to which the investigation contributes to the implementation of a broader government policy;
- enhanced constitutionality;
- whether the issues would be of interest to the private sector from which the broader community would also derive a benefit;
- whether the investigation would require substantial, long-term commitment and fundamental review;
- whether extensive public or professional consultation would be necessary;
- whether circumstances indicate that the investigation needs to be conducted in an impartial manner where vested interests are present or where there are significant differences in views or objectives among various relevant entities;
- whether an investigation would promote informed public debate on future policy direction; and
- the extent to which the investigation would benefit poor and previously disadvantaged communities.

Although all the above criteria are considered, a request need not meet all the secondary criteria to be included in the programme. Any proposal approved by the South African Law Reform Commission for investigation is submitted to the Minister of Justice and Constitutional Development and is included in the Commission's research programme after approval by this minister.

Some law reform agencies take a somewhat different approach to 'importance'. In the criteria published by the Australian Law Reform Commission and the Law Reform Commission of Tanzania, importance is explicitly linked to community concerns or the needs of the community. In South Australia, importance is linked to the administration of justice in the state, and in New Zealand the minister responsible for the Law Commission may require the Commission to accord priority to a project that fits within the government's priorities. The South Australian Law Reform Institute also gives independent weight to the priorities of the state's attorney-general.[21]

Many agencies also refer to the general needs of the programme, either as part of the 'resources' heading (for example, the Scottish Law Commission) or as a freestanding criterion (such as the Alberta Law Reform Institute).[22] Other criteria may also be added to this standard core. The Australian Law Reform Commission, for instance, refers to the need to update the law as a result of scientific or technological developments. The Tanzanian Commission makes express reference to time frame, requiring projects to be completed within two years.

3.6 Relations with government

Government support for the project is very important, and essential if legislation is required to implement the outcome.

For most standard model law reform agencies, governments are closely involved with the initiation of projects. References, where this mechanism is used, by definition involve an issue of concern to government. Even in respect of programmes, the statute establishing the law reform agency will generally require the programme to be at least approved by the government or a specified minister or law officer. More so, in-government law reform units can be expected to follow government priorities.

The position is different for institute model law reform agencies. However, most law reform institutes will include the attorney-general as an *ex officio* board member, or their nominees, who may express a government view during the process of drawing up a programme.

Whatever the formal position, the purpose of law reform is to change the law, not merely the academic purpose of setting out what a better law might be. So in all cases, it is unlikely to be a good use of law reform resources to start a law reform

New Zealand: Guiding executive referrals

The New Zealand Cabinet has set criteria for ministers to consider before proposing projects for the Law Commission's work programme. The criteria are contained in the Cabinet Office Circular (which is a binding directive on ministers and officials). Projects proposed for the Law Commission should meet one or more of the following criteria:

- involve issues that span the interests of a number of government agencies and professional groups;
- require substantial, long-term commitment or fundamental review;
- involve extensive public or professional consultation;
- need to be done independently of central government agencies because of the existence of vested interests, or a significant difference of views;
- require independent consideration in order to promote informed public debate on future policy direction;
- involve technical law reform of what is often called 'lawyer's law' that would be likely otherwise to escape attention.

project that the government opposes, or indeed to which the government is merely indifferent. Government buy-in to a project is always essential where the objective of the project is, as is usually the case, the implementation of reform by means of legislation.

It is therefore important, when considering initiating a law reform project, that the law reform agency discusses the proposed project with the relevant government ministry or ministries, and ensures that the government's view is considered as a factor in the decision-making process. Clear opposition from government will frequently be a deciding factor. However, such discussions are not all one way. If there is a strong case for a project, evidenced, for instance, by the concerns of civil society stakeholders, then the programme-making process can provide an opportunity for a law reform agency to put the case for a project to the government.

Steps can be taken to set out more formally the relations between a law reform agency and government in relation to the initiation of projects. In New Zealand, this has been accomplished through authoritative administrative guidance.

As discussed previously, the process of engagement with government generally has been taken a stage further in England and Wales, through the recent innovation of statutory protocols between the Law Commission for England and Wales and the

England and Wales: Initiation and the protocols

The statutory protocols between the two governments and the Law Commission seek to ensure that the relevant policy department is committed to the project from the outset.

The United Kingdom minister who approves the Law Commission's programme is the Lord Chancellor and Secretary of State for Justice. The protocol with the United Kingdom Government specifies that:

'Where the Commission is considering including a project in a Commission programme, the Commission will notify the Minister with relevant policy responsibility. In deciding how to respond to the Commission, the Minister will bear in mind that, before approving the inclusion of the project in the overall programme, the Lord Chancellor will expect the Minister (with the support of the Permanent Secretary):

1. to agree that the department will provide sufficient staff to liaise with the Commission during the currency of the project (normally, a policy lead, a lawyer and an economist); and

2. to give an undertaking that there is a serious intention to take forward law reform in this area.'

The protocol with the Welsh Government makes equivalent provision, taking into account that the Welsh Government does not approve the programme, unlike the Lord Chancellor.

United Kingdom Government (in respect of England) and the Welsh Government.

The reform that introduced the protocol was at the request of the Law Commission, and arose out of a concern with implementation rates of law reform projects. It illustrates the fact that approval by the Lord Chancellor had, in respect of England, not proved a sufficient guarantee that government was committed to the project at the outset.

The social, economic, cultural and technological issues facing a jurisdiction will impact the selection of law reform projects. Some challenges are global, such as the impact of technology on the law.

3.7 The contemporary context

All projects are selected in a context provided by the particular social, economic, cultural and technological issues facing each jurisdiction. The general political setting at any given time may therefore suggest the need for prioritising certain areas for review. A change of government can present a new series of reform priorities, some of which may become the basis for projects in a law reform agency work programme, or provide opportunities for implementation.

Ireland and austerity

Following the economic and financial crisis that emerged in the Republic of Ireland in 2008, the International Monetary Fund/European Union Financial Assistance Agreement for Ireland (2010) imposed a number of reform conditions as a standard feature of such assistance programmes. These included reform of the law concerning personal insolvency and on alternative dispute resolution. The Law Reform Commission of Ireland had, however, completed reviews in these areas, avoiding the need for external solutions.

The contemporary economic or financial position of a state or territory may also be significant. In recent decades, many jurisdictions have experienced economic shocks, which can in turn lead to externally mandated reform programmes, often linked to external financial assistance programmes. Externally mandated reform programmes, however, may not always be designed in the context of the affected state, and can be difficult to implement. By contrast, there are benefits in an indigenous

Democracy and development in South Africa

In preparation for the onset of South Africa's democracy in 1994, the South African Law Reform Commission was requested to investigate the protection of human rights and different constitutional models. The Commission conducted research into group and human rights and constitutional models as part of Project 58 (Group and Human Rights) and Project 77 (Constitutional Models). This research was considered in drafting the Constitution of the Republic of South Africa Act 200 of 1993, which in turn informed the drafting of the Constitution of the Republic of South Africa Act, 1996. Since then, the Commission has conducted a number of investigations that flowed from the requirements of the constitution. The latter includes an investigation into the harmonisation of the common law and indigenous law (Project 90: Customary Law), which resulted in the adoption of two statutes (the Recognition of Customary Marriages Act 120 of 1998 and the Reform of Customary Law of Succession and Regulation of Related Matters Act 11 of 2009); a review of the administrative law (Project 115: Review of Administrative Law), which resulted in the adoption of the Promotion of Administrative Justice Act 3 of 2000; and an investigation focusing on the rights to equality and human dignity in the context of domestic partnerships (Project 118: Domestic Partnerships), some of the recommendations of which were incorporated into the Civil Unions Act 17 of 2006.

The involvement of the Law Reform Commission in South Africa's development continues. South Africa has committed itself to achieving the goals set in its National Development Plan by the year 2030.[23] It seeks to address the triple scourge of poverty, inequality and unemployment. Areas in need of review, which speak to the aims of the National Development Plan, are given priority when considering the inclusion of projects in the Commission's law reform programme.

law reform agency putting forward proposals for reform that are consistent with the content of such external reform programmes.

Equally, the context in which law reform agencies work can include historic transformational change, to which the agency may contribute. Few changes in recent history were as significant as the process that led to the introduction of democracy in South Africa from 1990.

Challenges and opportunities of these sorts will vary from region to region and from jurisdiction to jurisdiction. However, some issues may be global. One such issue is the evolving impact of information technology and artificial intelligence on law and lawyers.

Law reform agencies may wish to consider to what extent they might include, within their work programmes, how legal frameworks may be affected by, and seek to regulate, such areas. Agencies may need to take account, for example, of a number of developments that may emerge over the coming years, including:[24]

- exponential growth in information communication technologies and connected devices;
- increasingly capable machines, with many tasks that currently require human beings being performed by machines, including professional services such as legal services, through a combination of:
  - big data analytics: already being used, for example, in e-discovery in civil and criminal trials, and for searching online legislation databases;
  - artificial intelligence and machine learning;
  - the integration of computing in everyday objects, such as driverless cars, and associated issues of liability for road traffic-related personal liability claims and criminal liability; and
  - affective computing systems that can detect and express emotions;
- distributed computing based on 'blockchain' systems, and their use in banking, payment and financial services, including the growth of virtual currencies such as Bitcoin.

These developments will likely give rise to many issues for law reform agencies. Among them are the following:

- online courts and the e-filing of documents;
- the use of information technology by judges in analysing questions of law;
- data analytics ('big data') and the civil and criminal justice system, including e-discovery;
- the application of existing data protection concepts in distributed data processing systems;
- freedom of speech, defamation and social media;
- cybercrime and cybersecurity regulation; and
- the regulation of artificial intelligence systems and machine learning tools.

Traditional law reform and statutory consolidation projects will remain a key element of law reform agency programmes into the foreseeable future. However, the impact of information communication technologies and artificial intelligence on substantive law and legal processes will likely become increasingly significant in many future-oriented law reform agency work programmes.

Notes

1 https://www.scotlawcom.gov.uk/files/9712/8014/6403/Report%20on%20 presumption%20of%20death%20Report%2034.pdf
2 http://www.lawreform.ie/news/report-on-civil-law-of-missing-persons. 388.html
3 South African Law Reform Commission, Project 137, Report on the review of the expungement of certain criminal records, 2017.
4   South African Law Reform Commission Project 84, Report on application of the trapping system, 1994.
5 http://salawreform.justice.gov.za/reports/r_pr110_01_2002dec.pdf
6 http://www.alrc.gov.au/report-16 and http://www.alrc.gov.au/report-20
7 https://www.gov.uk/government/publications/the-law-commission-report-on-criminal-code-for-england-and-wales-april-1989
8 https://www.scotlawcom.gov.uk/files/5712/8024/7006/cp_criminal_code. pdf
9 https://www.lawcom.gov.uk/project/sentencing-code/
10 https://www.bcli.org/project/strata-property-law-phase-one   and   http:// www.bcli.org/project/strata-property-law-phase-two. Strata property is a statutory form of property holding in which individuals own an interest in their own home and are members of a strata corporation which owns common parts, and has obligations in relation to maintenance, etc.
11 http://www.klrc.go.ke/index.php/bills/505-model-laws-developed-by-klrc

12 http://www.alrc.gov.au/publications/report-31

13 http://www.lawcom.govt.nz/our-projects/juries

14 Appendix B of a report of the Law Reform Commission of Ireland (2016) contains consultations with young people on harmful internet communications including cyber bullying.

15 The Northern Ireland Law Commission, while still formally in existence, has effectively been de-funded by the Northern Ireland Executive.

16 https://consultations.justice.govt.nz/independent/search-and-surveillance-act/

17 http://www.lawcom.gov.uk/about/how-we-work/

18 http://www.scotlawcom.gov.uk/files/6414/2321/6887/Ninth_Programme_of_Law_Reform_ Scot_Law_Com_No_242.pdf

19 Victorian Law Reform Commission Act 2000, section 5; http://www.lawreform.vic.gov.au/all-projects/about-community-law-reform/criteria-for-project

20 South African Law Reform Commission Thirty-Sixth Annual Report 2008/2009 11-12 (http://salawreform.justice.gov.za/anr/2008-09_anr.pdf)

21 http://www.alrc.gov.au/law-reform-process (Australia); the 2012–2013 annual report of the Law Reform Commission of Tanzania; https://law.adelaide.edu.au/research/law-reform-institute/ (South Australia); http://www.lawcom.govt.nz/sites/default/files/corporatePaperAttachments/NZLC%20Statement%20of%20Intent%202013-2016.pdf (New Zealand).

22 http://www.scotlawcom.gov.uk/files/6414/2321/6887/Ninth_Programme_of_Law_Reform_Scot_Law_Com_No_242.pdf (Scotland); https://www.alri.ualberta.ca/index.php/about-alri/our-process/project-selection (Alberta).

23 www.gov.za/issues/national-development-plan-2030

24 See for instance Susskind and Susskind 2015.

Chapter 4

The Planning and Management of Projects

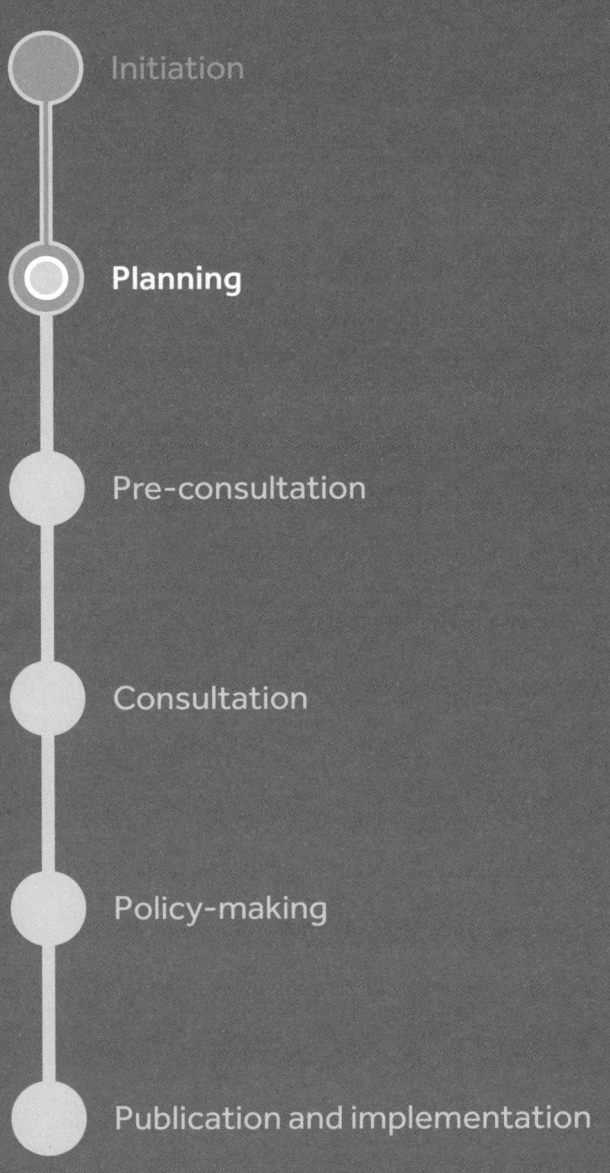

Initiation

Planning

Pre-consultation

Consultation

Policy-making

Publication and implementation

Chapter 4
The Planning and Management of Projects

Chapter 4 considers the planning and management of projects. It starts by looking at how project teams are formed, and then considers the basic elements of project management – a timeline and a budget; evaluation of progress; co-ordination of inputs; and risk management. The chapter goes on to discuss key mechanisms for project management. These include task lists, the identification of responsibilities, dependencies and timelines.

All law reform agencies plan and manage their projects. However, project planning is now a much more developed practice than it was in the early days of law reform. In many jurisdictions, the expectations that governments and other stakeholders have of law reform agencies have increased, particularly in relation to timetables.

Issues of personnel, timelines and budget, evaluation of progress, participant input and risk assessment will affect the planning and management of projects.

Project planning is a management discipline in its own right. There is a wide range of literature and many software packages are available. Providers offer project planning training, including in relation to specific software. Such training may well be helpful to the law reformer. But not all training will be relevant to the law reform context, and both training and software should be critically assessed to ensure that each is appropriate.

In reviewing approaches to planning and management of projects, this chapter anticipates discussion of the stages of a law reform project covered in the following chapters.

4.1 The starting point: the project team

Project planning starts with the choice that the law reform agency makes about how to constitute a team that will be charged with the conduct of the project. The structure of teams

Project teams: Three law reform agencies

Tanzania: Where the Law Reform Commission takes up a reference or proposal, a project team comprising a commissioner or commissioners and legal officers is constituted. The Commission co-opts external experts where necessary. The project team is responsible for analysing and identifying the issue and challenges for reform. The project team also sets estimated time frames for the review, and prepares a planning base and the budget needed for the review; there is also an economist. Subject to the planning exercise, the team then takes responsibility for the conduct of the enquiry. The Commission typically works on three projects at a time.

Australia: The federal-level Australian Law Reform Commission works solely on the basis of references from the government, which typically include a reporting date. There will usually be two projects running at the same time. One or two commissioners will be placed in charge of a project, with four or five legal staff making up the balance of the project team, along with a project assistant. The research manager and librarian will work with both projects. The staff and commissioners have sufficient expertise to cover most projects, supplemented by additional training if necessary, but sometimes a specialist consultant will be engaged.

England and Wales: The Law Commission has four standing law reform teams, each working under a commissioner, and covering different areas of law – currently, commercial and common law; criminal law; property, family and trust law; and public law. Each usually has between three and five lawyers and the same number of research assistants under a team manager, who is a more senior lawyer. The standard approach is to assign each project full time to a lawyer and a research assistant, with support from the team manager and commissioner, and other professionals at appropriate times, such as an economist and communications professionals. Legislative drafters are usually involved in the final months of the project, writing draft legislation based on the instructions of the team lawyer/research assistant.

For some projects, where the scope of the project is particularly wide or the timescale is short, the project team will be made up of more than one lawyer/research assistant.

Generally, each team has a core of permanent government lawyers. Other lawyers with particular expertise in a relevant subject may be recruited on time-limited contracts. Research assistants are recruited for a year from new law graduates.

The Commission runs multiple projects at the same time. In 2014/2015, there were 21 ongoing projects and eight final reports. In 2015/2016, the corresponding figures were 17 and four, respectively.

varies among law reform agencies. Most will have a standard pattern from which departures may be made if a particular project warrants it.

4.2 Elements of project management

The first core element of project management for law reform agencies comprises a timeline and a budget. It is likely that, in most jurisdictions, for most projects, the end point of the timetable will have been agreed with government.

The project timeline, in whatever form it is produced, will set out how the project will achieve the final date agreed.

Timetables

In Australia, federal government references of projects to the Australian Law Reform Commission from government ministers include a reporting date. The amount of time allowed for a project varies according to the size of the project, but a reporting date a year after the reference is common.

In England and Wales, the statutory protocols with the United Kingdom and Welsh Governments specify that, at the outset, the overall timescale for the project will be agreed between the Commission and government. As with all law reform agencies, project length varies a great deal, but an approximate standard timescale for an average project that includes the drafting of a bill is three years.

The budget indicates the resources available to the project. Different law reform agencies will have different accounting practices, and there is no necessity for a specific project to be an accounting centre, with its own budget expressed in monetary terms. In England and Wales, for instance, even the law reform teams, each of which will have several projects, do not have disaggregated monetary budgets. But the resources available are agreed in terms of staff inputs as part of the prioritisation inherent in the project initiation process.

The second key element is the evaluation of progress. The timeline will set out the key stages in the project, such as the publication of an issues paper; then the publication of a discussion paper or a single consultation paper; the close of consultation on, the production and/or publication of the analysis of responses; the production of a policy paper, if that is the practice of the law reform agency; and final report publication. There will be a system to evaluate progress with regard to each key milestone. Failure to meet a milestone will require justification and remedial action.

The third key element involves co-ordinating the input of a variety of participants. These include both internal and external participants. Internally, different resources may be utilised for the project at different times. Those resources need to be available at the right time. It is important in managing each individual project that the needs of potentially competing projects or other activities are programmed in. If, in a bill-drafting agency, several projects will require the services of legislative drafters at the same time, the projects may have to be staggered or more drafters may have to be obtained from the legislative drafting office. Publications, whether project-related or corporate, such as annual reports, must be staggered to take account of the capacity of those charged with the technical business of organising printing and press relations.

Equally, external participants – members of advisory groups, government policy officials and consultees in general – need to be aware of when and how to input into the project, and the processing of their input must be planned for and accommodated.

Fourthly, risks to the process must be managed. All projects can and will be affected by factors outside the control of the law reform agency. A change of government or minister, a negative consultation response from an important body, an unexpected outcome of a pending appeal or the loss of a key member of staff may all have adverse effects on a project. Project planning involves anticipating risks and taking steps to mitigate them.

4.3 Project planning mechanisms

Four aspects of project planning must always be considered: tasks, responsibilities, dependencies and timelines. Each of these should be mapped in detail, accounting for contingencies, variables and risks.

This section considers four aspects of project planning: tasks, responsibility, dependencies and timelines. There are many formal approaches to project management, including those based on particular project planning software. Many law reform agencies have developed their own tailored approaches to the functions involved. Rather than recommend particular packages or approaches, the broad mechanisms necessary for project management are set out below.

4.3.1 Tasks

The core of a project plan will include a number of tasks, each with increasing specificity as the relevant staff member details each of the phases of the typical law reform project. The exact content of tasks will depend on the structure of projects in that law reform agency and the stage of the task within the project under consideration. Guidance on these will be apparent from the stage-specific chapters of this guide. There should always, however, be some considered plan that sets out tasks and sub-tasks down to the level of specificity so that every member of the project teams knows what they are expected to do, and by when.

Broadly, the more specific the task list is, the more reliable the plan will be. It takes time to generate task lists. But it is important to do so. In the first place, it inevitably saves more time later if the task is programmed carefully in advance. Secondly, accurate, realistic and flexible task lists are invaluable in allowing the project manager to estimate the time and resources necessary for each stage of the project, and ultimately the project as a whole.

One way of generating the task list is for each staff member to document what they do in the course of the day or week in some detail. The resulting record provides a description of the process each person goes through and the tasks that they perform.

Alberta: Meetings in a multi-track project

The Alberta Law Reform Institute undertook a project to re-write the province's out-of-date Rules of Civil Procedure.[1] The reformed rules came into effect in 2010. The multi-year project, initially estimated to cost C$2.6 million, involved almost 24 full-time or part-time counsel. There were 11 working groups, a steering committee and a drafting committee, amounting to 118 volunteers. In total, the project accounted for in excess of 30,000 person hours. The 11 different working groups examined subjects from the commencement of actions to discovery and evidence to management of litigation. The project produced issues papers and 21 consultation documents over a five-year period.

With 11 working groups and two other major committees, involving members from the two major urban centres in the province and others across the province, many meetings were held. Organising these meetings effectively was a particularly important element of the project, and the project team developed a detailed task list/checklist for meetings. The following is a very small extract from the overall project document:

Meeting arrangement procedures:

- canvass for dates
- confirm date
- prepare meeting summary sheet
- book facility (video teleconference)
- email meeting dates to committee members
- order food
- send a reminder notice (a few days prior)
- contact facility with the number attending and the caterer
- agenda:
    - prepare draft agenda
    - gather materials for agenda
    - format materials and finalise agenda
    - duplicate for paper copy recipients
    - distribute agenda and materials
- post-meeting procedures:
    - distribute minutes with the next meeting material
    - email minutes to other counsel
    - check catering expenses are correct.

4.3.2 Responsibilities

If the identification of tasks is important, then assigning responsibility is critical. Who will perform the task, certify it is complete, and move the project along to the next stage?

Responsibility takes several forms. The person performing the task may certify that it is complete, or may report to another whose job it is to co-ordinate the completion of an array of tasks. A publications manager may receive reports from a lawyer to confirm that content is correct; from an administrative assistant to confirm that formatting is complete; from an intern to confirm that footnotes have been checked. All of these confirmations certify that the report may now be published on the website. The chair/director will require reports from others on the stages of completion and the budget status of various projects in order to have a meaningful discussion with funders or legislators.

Large organisations will often have significant resources devoted to quality assurance. Many law reform agencies are small or medium sized and may not be able to devote resources exclusively to quality assurance and risk management. However, a clear delineation of an understanding of responsibilities will help to avoid errors when staff are faced with heavy workloads.

One of the most effective ways of ensuring that responsibilities are handled effectively is the progress meeting. Such meetings can be regularly scheduled, but kept short and focused on those who need to know and those who need to report.

Responsibility and accountability can go hand-in-hand in a positive way.

4.3.3 Dependencies

This concept introduces an element of complexity into the more straightforward identification of tasks and assignments of responsibility. Even if the project is thought of as progressing through sequential stages, they will often overlap, in that preparation for the next stage can and should begin before the previous stage is complete. For example, if a working group is to be used, the members can be identified, their time and availability confirmed and their contact information set up – all in advance of and in anticipation of the first meeting. Procedures and expectations can be set out in the invitation and confirming correspondence. The actual timing of the working group

Accountability against project milestones: England and Wales

In England and Wales, there is a full commissioners' meeting every two weeks, at which draft publications and policy papers are agreed. Every other meeting, the commissioners constitute, along with the chief executive, the programme board, and are joined by the non-executive director (currently the head of a British university and a former permanent secretary in a government ministry). At programme board meetings, the team managers of each of the four law reform teams report on progress against milestones on each of the teams' law reform projects. Every three months, there is an expanded programme board meeting that considers a more detailed report from each team that concentrates on forward-looking adjustments to the project plan.

Each board report assesses progress against milestones, making use of a 'red–amber–green' system to indicate the level of risk to a particular milestone. The example below shows the progress of projects of the Commercial and Common Law team:

Commercial and Common Law					
Project	Milestones	By date	Commissioners' Meeting	RAG (May)	RAG (Apr)
Transfer/event Fees in Retirement Homes and Other Leases	• Interim Report Published • Final Report to be published			GREEN	GREEN
Implementation: Groundless Threats	• Implementation			GREEN	GREEN
Bills of sale: drafting new Goods Mortgages Act	• Report and draft Bill	September 2017	Various – TBC	AMBER	AMBER
Insurable Interest	• Consultation on updated Bill	Late 2017	TBC	AMBER	AMBER
Social investments and pensions	• Final Report	June 2017	11 May 2017	AMBER	AMBER

Issues:	**Event Fees**: Published on 30 March (5 working days ahead of schedule). **Intellectual Property (Unjustified Threats)**: The Bill received Royal Assent on 27 April 2017. **Goods Mortgages Act**: We have been working to an extremely tight timetable to meet Parliamentary deadlines. The election has affected the timetable further and an alternative timetable may be required. **Insurable Interest**: On 18 Oct Commissioners confirmed postponement of insurable interest pending completion of social pensions' project. **Social pensions**: The team is preparing a blackline draft to circulate to Commissioners, incorporating Commissioners' written comments and feedback at the peer review meeting on 11 May. A draft summary will follow. We have shared individual chapters with key stakeholders and are responding to their comments.
Decisions:	Board to discuss potential new timetable for the Goods Mortgages Act.

commencement is dependent on the completion of the materials for consideration, the preparation of a work plan and an agenda.

Not to do this preparatory work would unnecessarily lengthen the timelines and create downtime. On the other hand, artificially accelerating the timeline may compromise material preparation and reduce the quality of the working group output and advice. There may also be internal dependencies. Staff lawyers may be working on more than one project at a time. Some of the responsibilities can be compartmentalised, but intense analysis or report writing may require exclusive dedicated time until completion. Especially in smaller agencies, these pressures must be taken into account.

4.3.4 Timelines

Estimating the length of time required for each stage in a law reform project, and ultimately the length of the entire project, is a key requirement of law reform planning.

Experience will give the law reform agency a broad sense of the average total length of most projects. An overall figure may provide a useful check at the end of the process. However, it does not take account of the particular challenges of the project under consideration. Projects vary according to factors such as their size, complexity and the difficulty or otherwise of the consultation process. Account must also be taken of internal factors such as staff or commissioner turnover and budget uncertainty.

A reliable time estimate will be based on a realistic assessment of the time to be taken for each component part of the project. A law reform agency may well have a standard timetable that can be consulted, but in each case adjustments must be made to the standard timetable to take account of the particular challenges of the project being planned.

Estimates should allow for both the amount of effort and the duration of time within which the effort is to be expended. A project lawyer may have accurately estimated that 15 days' work is needed to complete a particular task. In assessing the duration of the task, however, other things must be taken into account. The lawyer will inevitably have other routine matters to attend to, such as staff meetings, correspondence on past projects and line management meetings. It may be known that the lawyer will be expected to spend two or three days assisting in relation to an event planned for another project. The outcome may be that the 15 days' work is likely to be completed within a period of 25 days.

It is important that time, both in terms of effort and duration, is managed effectively so that other activities that depend on the completion of certain tasks are not delayed. Estimates are not immune from abuse – they can be grossly exaggerated in terms of effort and time for completion so that no task is ever completed late. On the other hand, being too ambitious imposes unnecessary pressure to complete the task or compromises the quality or the reliability of the work.

It is important, therefore, for this sort of time estimate to be reviewed by those in a position to provide informed questioning or challenge, for instance a commissioner or a more senior staff member.

A timeline must take account of contingencies, variables and risks.

The project planner will know that a variable exists, but not what the outcome will be. If a decision goes one way, little further work will be needed. If the decision goes the other way, a new work programme will be needed. The timeline must allow for both possible outcomes.

A contingency, on the other hand, is an indeterminacy that is not known in advance. Experience shows that in any complex project there is a high probability that something will occur that will mean extra time is necessary. It may be that a major consultation group needs additional time to finalise its response, that a member of staff leaves unexpectedly, that a development in the law must be accommodated or simply that research reveals a new and complicated aspect that had not been anticipated. It is therefore wise to build in some leeway for such events, either formally, by including an additional 10 per cent in each time period, for instance, or informally, by rounding up time estimates.

Thirdly, risk must be planned for. The example of a risk register from the Law Commission for England and Wales above illustrates the sort of risks that may be anticipated. In addition to each project having a risk register, the Commission develops and maintains a corporate risk register.

Each law reform agency may have its own formal or informal way of planning for risks. However it is done, the distinction

Review points

In some projects, review points may be agreed with the government ministry responsible for that area of the law. In 2008, the Law Commission for England and Wales started a project on adult social care. The project plan provided for two review points. The Law Commission and the United Kingdom Department of Health could agree to continue or discontinue the project at each review point. The initial phase of the project provided for a scoping exercise to delineate the issues to be covered by the substantive project. At the review point, both parties agreed that the project should continue. The second review point was after the publication of the substantive report, and its purpose was to decide on whether the Law Commission should go on to produce a draft bill for government consideration. At that point, both parties agreed that the Law Commission should not do so. The reason for this decision was the determination of the government to legislate for the project, and so prepare its own bill, which was later enacted as the Care Act 2011.

The project plan accommodated the decision-making variables at each stage.

between the likelihood of a risk occurring and the impact that the risk would have if it did come about provides a useful way of analysing risk. The purpose of thinking about risk in this way is to plan what can be done to minimise those risks. However, anticipating risk by taking countervailing measures itself uses up resources. The distinction between likelihood and impact assists with the consideration of how much resource should be devoted

Limiting the advance plan

Another way of dealing with future uncertainty, whether in terms of variables or contingencies, is to limit the determinate plan.

In 2015, the Alberta Law Reform Institute commenced a project on the rule against perpetuities, a highly technical issue in the law of trusts.[2] The following is an extract from the original time estimate/plan.

Project Design
1. OVERVIEW

   [4] It is proposed that this project follow the standard trajectory of Report for Discussion [RFD], consultation and Final Report [FR]. To focus discussion and input in this difficult area, ALRI should formulate preliminary recommendations in a formal RFD, rather than attempt to consult using open-ended questions in a more general consultation document.

   [5] At this stage, I have been asked to prepare the Preliminary Assessment only to the RFD stage. Therefore, no design or time estimates are yet being suggested for the consultation and FR stages. I am advised that further planning for those stages is best undertaken once the direction of ALRI's preliminary recommendations is clear.

2. MILESTONE DOCUMENTS

   [6] All targeted completion dates in this section assume a project commencement date of March 1, 2015.

- **Background Issues Memo** (includes reading and consideration of research already done, conducting further research as needed, analysis, writing of memo, presentation of memo to one Board meeting for formulation of preliminary recommendations)

  Targeted Board Meeting Date: June 26, 2015

- **Report for Discussion** (includes conversion of Background Issues Memo to RFD style, inclusion of preliminary recommendations, approval process of draft RFD by Board at one meeting, revisions, preparation for publication)

  Targeted Board Meeting Date: September 18, 2015

  Targeted Publication Date: October 15, 2015

The report for discussion was published in April 2016. The project continued, and a final report was published in March 2017.

to avoiding the risk. High-resource mitigation may not be called for if the risk is low, even if its impact would be very high if it did occur. On the other hand, it may be sensible to devote more resources to a risk with moderate impact, if it is much more likely to occur.

Notes

1 http://www.assembly.ab.ca/lao/library/egovdocs/2008/alilr/171319.pdf (final report); http://www.cfcj-fcjc.org/inventory-of-reforms/alberta-rules-of-court-project (links to other publications).
2 https://www.alri.ualberta.ca/index.php/completed-projects/rule-against-perpetuities

Chapter 5

Pre-consultation:
Research and Drafting

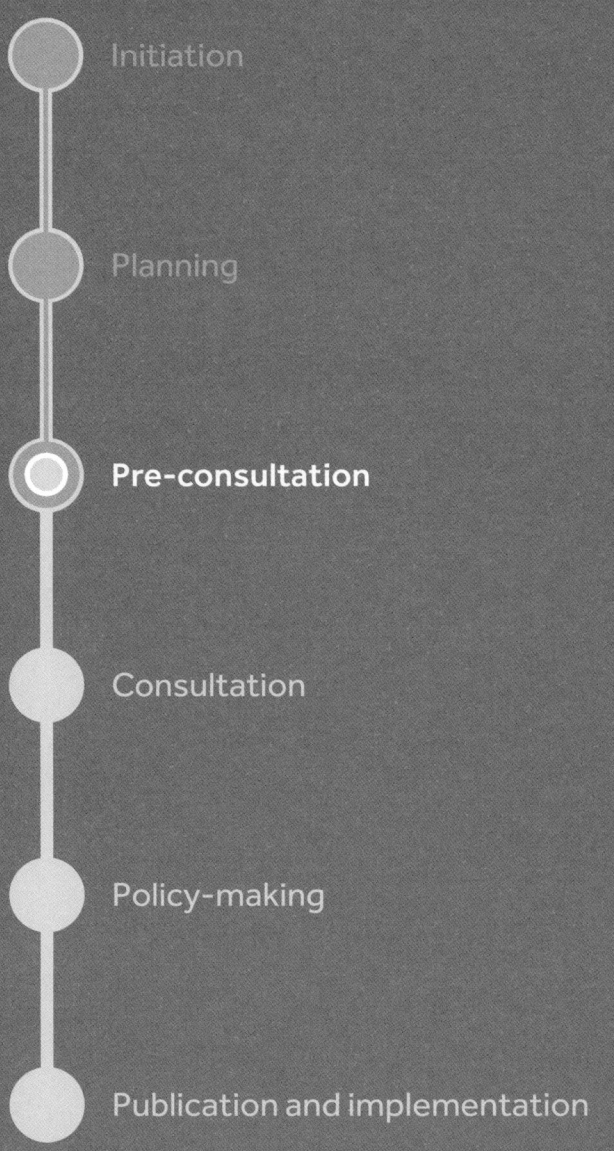

Initiation

Planning

Pre-consultation

Consultation

Policy-making

Publication and implementation

Chapter 5
Pre-consultation: Research and Drafting

Chapter 5 considers the first stage of a law reform project – research and drafting in the period before the start of consultation. A variety of first stage documents are examined, including documents that provide background, analysis and initial conclusions for consultation. The chapter considers legal research, as practised in law reform agencies. This means not only research into the law, and its development within the jurisdiction, but also comparative legal research and empirical social science research. The chapter then considers the nature and value of pre-consultation engagement with stakeholders. It provides guidance on the drafting of consultation documents and the development of legal policy in a consultation document, as well as the balance between provisional proposals and questions.

The first substantive stage of any law reform project is preparation for consultation. This involves initial research on the law, and on the social and economic context, with a view to the drafting of documents to support the consultation process. Occasionally, law reform agencies may undertake work that does not require consultation. However, these are rare, and usually the first stage involves researching and drafting a first stage document for use in consultation.

The first stage of a project is usually the researching and drafting of a first stage document, for use in consultation. These documents provide background material, descriptive information, preliminary analysis or an initial scoping of the law reform task at hand.

5.1 First stage documents

The nomenclature of first stage documents varies between law reform agencies globally, and indeed within the same agency over time. The documents are variously referred to as research papers, background papers, working papers, preliminary papers, information papers, consultation papers and issues papers. Although they may vary slightly in content, form and focus, they all serve the purpose of providing background material on the issue under review, descriptive information about the

The law reformer must take care to ensure that the consultation document is clearly written, well researched, and easily understood by the key audiences.

law as it stands, preliminary analysis and thinking about issues or problems raised, or an initial scoping of the law reform task at issue. Sometimes a single document is used to inform a single consultation stage. At other times, or for other projects, a law reform agency may publish an initial, more open paper or papers followed by a further document including reform proposals.

The type of the initial document produced may depend on factors such as the time frame set for an inquiry, the available resources and the way in which a law reform body is constituted – in particular, whether it can self-refer or act only on terms of reference from government. In situations where time frames are tight, it may not be practical to produce

Three Australasian approaches

The Australian Law Reform Commission works to terms of reference and strict timelines of, on average, 12 months to the final report. The first document that is most commonly produced is an issues paper. This document presents the Australian Law Reform Commission's initial analysis of the terms of reference and provides an outline of the legal issues identified as being problematic and needing reform. It represents the Australian Law Reform Commission's preliminary thinking on the subject and asks open questions about the community's experience of the area under review, seeking advice about any issues that may have been missed, and asking for feedback on the initial scoping and analysis. It opens the conversation with the community and invites their participation in the process. It often suggests or outlines principles that could guide proposals or provide a framework for reform and asks the community for guidance on these. Usually, stakeholders will have around eight weeks to respond to the issues paper during which time the Australian Law Reform Commission will continue its research and analysis and also proactively consult.

In other cases, an agency may, in considering whether to investigate a particular area of law, commission background or research papers to collect data and an evidence base on the need for reform, or to canvass the issues prior to settling specific terms of reference.

The Victorian Law Reform Commission produced four information papers for its inquiry into victims of crime to provide background information about the history of the modern criminal trial and its underlying principles, evidence about who victims are and what they need from the criminal justice system, information about the International Criminal Court as a case study of victim participation and a review of the sources of victims' rights internationally and in Australia. Three months later it then produced a consultation paper that sought public submissions.

The New Zealand Law Commission produces issues papers for consultation on its references. On rare occasions, the Commission has produced a study paper as a way of informing discussion on a reference. For example, in 2007 it produced a study paper that set out some privacy concepts and issues to assist stakeholders in conceptualising law reform issues in this area.

Initial documents

The Law Commission for England and Wales sometimes produces what it refers to as scoping reports. These may be produced when the Commission has agreed to take on a project, but the exact scope of the endeavour requires more precise definition. Scoping papers are generally published for information, rather than inviting consultation. Such exercises may be preliminary to further government commitment to a project, and can involve further decisions. For example, the Law Commission's scoping paper on adult social care required approval by the government, and one element of the scope that the Commission proposed, namely that adjudication of disputes be included, was rejected by the government. A project then proceeds to a further paper on which consultation takes place.

The Singapore Law Reform and Revision Division of the Attorney-General's Chambers produces consultation papers that include questions about whether the law should be reformed and how, and call for the community to make submissions to the inquiries. In some cases, it also publishes information papers providing background and explaining the issues.

In order to actively involve the community at an early stage, the South African Law Reform Commission also publishes issues papers for appropriate investigations as the first step in the consultation process. These papers announce an investigation, describe the aim and extent of the investigation, point to possible options available for solving existing problems, and initiate and stimulate debate on identified issues by way of including specific questions on relevant issues.

background or information papers, and organisations may need instead to go straight to a consultation paper or issues paper.

In many cases, the first document in a law reform project will be the consultation document, with which the law reform agency will seek to engage the relevant community. However, there may also be other documents produced as part of an initial, definitional stage.

As the process for each law reform project may differ slightly according to the scope of the inquiry, the range of stakeholders, the complexity of the laws under review and the period of time allotted for the inquiry, the initial documents produced will vary. However, they commonly offer the first point of engagement with the community in the law reform process in question. It is therefore important to ascertain which form of document will best serve these purposes. These documents also serve to manage stakeholder expectations about what the inquiry might achieve, what it might focus on and, importantly, what might be considered outside of the terms of reference and scope. Whatever the decision about first documents, whether

Enhancing accessibility

Since its Disability Inquiry in 2014, the Australian Law Reform Commission makes its issues papers available in 'Easy English' for greater accessibility, and produces summaries in 20 community languages. In line with Welsh Government guidelines, the Law Commission for England and Wales publishes some consultation papers and reports in both Welsh and English.

they are issues papers or scoping papers, consultation papers or discussion papers, the key is to be aware of the audience that the document is written for, and what the purpose of the document is. Consultation lies at the heart of most law reform processes and is important for developing effective recommendations because good law reform and effective implementation depend on involving the people who may be affected by it and taking their views into account.

Care must be taken with the form of consultation papers, to ensure that they are appropriately accessible to the appropriate audiences. For example, it may be necessary to publish a paper in more than one language.

Particular steps may be necessary to ensure that all members of the relevant community have access to papers. This may include ensuring that papers are available in audio or large print forms for people with visual disabilities, or easy read versions to make them accessible to people with learning difficulties. It may also be very helpful to consultees to prepare a summary of the paper.

Extensive community and stakeholder engagement is intrinsic to independent law reform, a topic covered in detail in the next chapter. First documents provide a key starting place in this process of community engagement and it is important that they are well researched, clearly written, accessible and set the right tone for the inquiry going forward in whatever form they take.

5.2 Legal research

Legal research remains the key to law reform consultation and similar documents.

All good law reform depends on high-quality research. The type of research undertaken and resources available will vary from one law reform agency to another. The scope and depth of any research proposed should be carefully planned in advance, including the timescales, and the research envisaged should be proportionate to the nature and purpose of the law reform project. The method of research and approach will depend on the agency that conducts the research, the time allotted, and the nature and breadth of the subject.

Research is fundamental. The nature of the research will depend on the goals of the reform.

The impetus for the reform may be driven by a variety of goals, such as:

- to increase efficiency and effectiveness;
- to provide a technical fix;
- to reflect changing community views and attitudes;
- to give effect to international obligations;
- to respond to new economic and technological development; or
- to respond to constitutional challenges.

The nature of law reform research is coloured by these goals. It is therefore not primarily or purely an academic exercise. It is, rather, instrumental in nature. There are usually clear objectives and outcomes, which must be kept in mind and which will shape the direction and approach of the research. The idea that should therefore be kept in the forefront of the mind is that legal research for the purposes of law reform is always driven by the mandate of the agency to reform and modernise the law, to find solutions:

> [W]hen research is undertaken as part of the process of law reform, it is undertaken as a part of the process, it is undertaken with a definite end, namely making suggestions for improvements in the law on concrete and easily identifiable matters and the formulation of those proposals in precise terms.[1]

It is necessary therefore to tailor the methods to be adopted – depending on the type of agency, the resources available, the time allotted and the subject – to the nature and extent of research. Where the law reform agency is a hybrid body or a government department, issues such as the needs of the administration may take precedence in the time allotted to meet objectives. More generally, the exigencies of working within government may provide other challenges for such agencies.

The internet has greatly expanded the scope and variety of legal research opportunities. The Commonwealth Secretariat, through its Office of Civil and Criminal Justice Reform, provides access to the Legal Knowledge Exchange Portal. This includes searchable national legislation from Commonwealth countries in selected legal areas.

5.2.1 The internet

The internet has transformed legal research. Prior to the explosion of information available on the internet, the best that could be hoped for was access to well-stocked libraries and contacts with universities, government departments, lawyers and law reform agencies in other countries in order to obtain books or copies of material. Information could be hard to come by and could take time to locate and obtain in physical form. This posed particular challenges for less well-resourced and smaller law reform agencies in developing countries.

Some key internet resources

Legal information institute websites exist in many parts of the world. Almost all of these institutes collect case law transcripts; many also provide legislation, treaties, law reform reports and other legal materials. Some, such as Austlii, the Australasian Legal Information Institute, also include some journals.

CommonLII, the Commonwealth Legal Information Institute, acts as a portal for eight Commonwealth Legal Information Institutes, covering 60 Commonwealth and other common law jurisdictions (some of which are mentioned in this box): http://www.commonlii. org/. Another general portal is the World Legal Information Institute: http://www.worldlii.org/.

Some examples of legal information institute websites are given below:

- Asia (http://www.asianlii.org/): includes some information on 30 national jurisdictions (not all include case law) and 13 Indian state jurisdictions.
- Australasia (http://www.austlii.edu.au/): all Australian jurisdictions and New Zealand. For New Zealand, see also http://www.nzlii.org/.
- British and Irish (http://www.bailii.org/): all United Kingdom jurisdictions, Ireland, Jersey, the European Union and the European Court of Human Rights. For Ireland, see also https://www.ucc.ie/law/irlii/index.php.
- Canada (https://www.canlii.org/): all Canadian jurisdictions.
- Hong Kong (http://www.hklii.org/eng/).
- Kenya (http://kenyalaw.org/kl/).
- Pacific Islands (http://www.paclii.org/): 20 Pacific islands, both Commonwealth and non-Commonwealth.
- Southern Africa (http://www.saflii.org/): 16 southern African states, including all South African jurisdictions.
- United Kingdom territories and dependencies (http://www.worldlii.org/catalog/3144.html): 14 jurisdictions.
- Cornell Law School's Legal Information Institute (https://www.law.cornell.edu/): includes information on US and state jurisdictions through links to relevant websites.

Apart from current subscription services such as LexisNexis and Westlaw, the proliferation of official government, parliamentary and court websites alongside those of law reform agencies from around the world, legal information institutes and other free web-based resources now make it possible to access a large volume of material from authoritative sources. This has provided a great opportunity for smaller law reform agencies to access necessary research material. In fact, the internet now poses the opposite challenge, with very large volumes of material published from a wide range of sources, not all of which may be updated or accurate.

Some key internet resources (cont.)

The Commonwealth Secretariat, http://www.thecommonwealth.org, through its Office of Civil and Criminal Justice Reform provides access to the Legal Knowledge Exchange Portal for member countries. This includes searchable national legislation from Commonwealth countries in selected legal areas, including constitutional law, criminal law, oceans and natural resource law, commercial law, and health and education law.

The three regional human rights regimes provide case law websites: http://en.african-court.org/ (African Court of Human and People's Rights); http://www.corteidh.or.cr/index.php/en (Inter-American Court of Human Rights); and http://www.echr.coe.int/Pages/home.aspx?p=home (European Convention on Human Rights). The Universal Human Rights Index is also useful: http://wwwuhri.ohchr.org.

Many national and sub-state authorities provide legislative websites, including:

- South African Government website of Federal legislation: http://www.gov.za/documents/acts;
- Database of Indian Federal legislation maintained by the Supreme Court Judges' Library: http://supnet.nic.in/legis/mainpage.html;
- Legislation by the United Kingdom Parliament and devolved legislatures in Scotland, Wales and Northern Ireland: http://www.legislation.gov.uk.[2]

Other relevant sources are:

- the American Law Institute: http://www.ali.org;
- the Asian Business Law Institute: http://wwwabli.asia;
- the Uniform Law Commission (The National Conference of Commissioners on Uniform State Laws): http://www.uniformlaws.org.

The initial task for a law reform researcher is to determine what the law is in their jurisdiction; what problems exist; what can be done to remedy those problems; and what the options for reform are and why.

Understanding what the law is involves researching the history of how and why the law came to be.

5.2.2 Types of research

Once the law reform subject has been assigned or determined and the issues to be addressed identified, the initial task of law reform researchers can be conveniently summarised as determining:

- what the law is in their jurisdiction;

- what problems or deficiencies exist;

- what can be done to remedy those problems; and

- what the options for reform are and why.

The initial issues to be addressed are usually clear from the terms of the reference or assignment, the subject matter and the circumstances that may have prompted the reference. It should be recognised however that research will often reveal other issues, directly relevant or collateral, which may also need to be addressed. The researcher must keep a balance between maintaining a focus on the primary concerns of the project and ensuring that all relevant matters are included.

5.2.3 What is the law of this jurisdiction?

The law reform agency is presented with a law reform issue that needs to be addressed. The issues or task may (or may not) be set out in a relatively clear, comprehensive manner. Determining what the law is in the jurisdiction will involve not only finding out what the law

---

Legal history and law reform

In 1996, the ancient common law 'year and a day rule' was abolished in England and Wales. The rule provided that a person can only be charged with an offence of homicide if the victim dies within a year and a day of the defendant's act or omission. The abolition of the rule (by section 1 of the Law Reform (Year and a Day Rule) Act 1996) was the result of a recommendation of the Law Commission for England and Wales in its report *Legislating the Criminal Code: The Year and a Day Rule in Homicide*.[3] The rule caused real problems with the adequate prosecution of crime. It was felt that it was inappropriate now that life support machines could keep victims alive well after the period had elapsed. Another problem was that in many cases there was no offence with which people could be charged if the injured person survived for more than a year and a day, which would otherwise have been gross negligence manslaughter. But a powerful element in the case for reform was made by considering the history of the rule from its thirteenth century origins, which demonstrated that it arose from obscure medieval procedural concerns, not as a matter of high principle. As such, it could be seen to be merely obsolescent and anachronistic.

is at the present time; that is, the existing state of the law, but also obtaining a picture of how the law came to be in its present state. This will often involve an investigation into the historical development of the law in order to understand the reasons behind the existing law, the course of its evolution and the factors that prompted changes to the law over time. The point is not to simply expound the law but to understand it, its origins, its rationale, its history and its application over time so as to be able to formulate recommendations for reform that will address the relevant issues with a better law.

5.2.4 Legislation

The researcher must find relevant statutes including subsidiary legislation, such as regulations, orders and rules. Care should be taken to ascertain that all the potentially relevant statutes are considered. In the larger jurisdictions in which they are available, internet services providing amended and annotated legislation may be invaluable. However, in many jurisdictions use must still be made of alphabetical lists of statutes, indexes and chronological tables. In most jurisdictions, case law will be relevant to the legislative regime. Again, in large jurisdictions, practitioner texts or academic works may be consulted. Where these are not available in smaller jurisdictions, such works published in larger allied jurisdictions may still be helpful, but must of course be used with caution.

Comprehensive research into the state of the law must include research into legislation, case law and secondary sources.

Where statutes have been amended and consolidated over time, care should be taken to ascertain that relevant parts of the statute have not been omitted or changed. Although the commercially available databases in some jurisdictions may be relied on, they may well not be available or reliable in relation to other jurisdictions.

The dangers of statutory amendment

In Jamaica, the antiquated Prisons Act and Commissioner of Corrections Act were replaced by a modern Corrections Act in 1985. The question then arose in 2015 of the status of Prisons Regulations 1980. The Corrections Act as passed in the Jamaican Parliament contained 87 sections. Section 87 made provision for repeals of previous Acts but also provided that regulations, licences, orders and rules made under the repealed Acts continued to have effect as if made under the new Corrections Act. Later, the Corrections Act was added to the official volumes of the Law of Jamaica and, as part of the law revision process, apparently spent provisions, such as section 87, were omitted. An examination of the Corrections Act would leave the researcher unclear on whether the Prisons Regulations 1980 were still in force, and without more research the conclusion might be drawn that these regulations were no longer in force.

It may therefore be critical that the historical development of the statute, where it has been amended, repealed and replaced, is investigated. Where legislation is available in searchable electronic databases, such as legal information institute and government websites, it may be possible to access point-in-time legislation to make the task easier.

Historical research may be important for three reasons. First, it may indicate why particular provisions were crafted in their present form and will supply some indication of the reasons that justified the particular approach. Secondly, it may reveal that alternatives may have been considered and rejected, and the reasons why they were rejected. Thirdly, this research may show that a provision that was relevant and justified at the time of its making is no longer justified.

The researcher will also need to be aware of other sources of rules and standards such as codes of conduct or practice that are mandated by the statutes that establish self-regulatory regimes for particular subjects or sectors. Examples include professional codes of conduct that apply to lawyers, medical doctors or industry codes of practice under data protection or protected disclosure (whistle-blowing) legislation.

5.2.5 Case law

Cases in which the relevant common law rule or statute has been litigated or prosecuted are a critical source for the researcher. This is particularly so where the judgment or opinion of the court interprets, applies, explains or comments on the issue. Attention must be paid to the hierarchy of courts. Care must be taken to ensure that principles of good case research are adhered to and to determine where cases have been overruled, reversed or distinguished.

It is important to remember that for law reform purposes important perspectives on the subject may be found in *obiter dicta* and dissenting opinions. A case may be important for law reform purposes for what was said by the court, rather than what was decided.

Whether statute or case law, the objective is always to provide a clear and comprehensive picture of the law in order to identify problems and deficiencies where the law reform task is a general review of the area of law, or to more precisely delineate and define the scope of the problem where the reference is a narrower one.

5.2.6 Other resources

Law reform researchers will also have recourse to standard secondary sources, such as:

- legal encyclopaedias such as *Halsbury's Laws of England/Australia/Canada*, *Laws of Scotland: Stair Memorial Encyclopaedia*, the *Canadian Encyclopaedic Digest* (Western and Ontario) and *Corpus Juris Secundum* (USA);

- legal text books;

- legal periodicals and journals;

- case digests, e.g. *The Digest* (United Kingdom); and

- legal dictionaries.

Consideration of these materials crosses over into the consideration below of comparative research, but their inclusion at this point reflects the reality that many jurisdictions will not have local versions of these works and, where issues relating to the common law are involved, much of this material remains relevant and useful for research of local law. In this regard, it may be that older, superseded volumes of these works may prove useful; even more so than up-to-date volumes.

Legal textbooks provide in-depth commentary and scholarly analysis of areas of law. They also provide footnotes with citations to potentially relevant cases, statutes and secondary authorities. Useful standard features include indexes and tables of cases, statutes and abbreviations.

Larceny v Theft

In England and Wales, the Theft Act 1968 replaced the previous law on larceny, much of which was contained in the Larceny Act 1861, and cases decided on that Act. The current edition of *Halsbury's Laws of England* therefore covers the law since the 1968 Theft Act. However, in a number of Commonwealth jurisdictions, the (in England and Wales) older law still obtains. Therefore, the third edition of *Halsbury's Laws of England*, published between 1952 and 1964, rather than the up-to-date version, is the key reference for the researcher in these jurisdictions.

Legal encyclopaedias are multi-volume sets that provide overviews and a detailed description of the law on a range of legal topics, usually those more often encountered in practice. In addition to reproducing much of the statute law and secondary legislation in a convenient form, their commentary provides references and footnotes to primary sources, including relevant cases and other legislation.

Journal articles tend to focus on narrower legal issues. The authors, usually academics and practitioners in a particular field, provide informed analysis of the law and references to relevant case law and legislation. Journal articles are especially useful for commentary on emerging areas of the law, and areas undergoing change.

Digests contain summaries of court cases. These collections of case digests are usually an attempt to provide the researcher with an exhaustive list of cases for a particular jurisdiction or subject area. Digests are arranged under broad subject headings and sub-headings.

In addition to these legal resources, there are many written resources dealing with the development or implementation of legislation, and the law more widely, which provide helpful explanation, comment and opinion. These include:

- records of parliamentary proceedings (called Hansard in the United Kingdom and some other jurisdictions);

- parliamentary committee reports;

- ministry papers (green papers/white papers);

- law reform agency reports;

- reports of commissions of inquiry;

- reports of advisory bodies, independent authorities and professional associations;

- non-legal academic writing/textbooks and peer-reviewed journals; and

- newspaper reports and articles.

In many Commonwealth jurisdictions, green papers are consultation documents produced by government ministries and departments to inform the public and to give the ministry or department feedback on its policy or legislative proposals. White papers are policy documents produced by the government that set out firm proposals for future legislation.

The records of proceedings of parliament (Hansard) are frequently useful for ascertaining the intent of the legislation and the policy, and the concerns that were the impetus for its introduction and passage. This is often critical in the analysis of the problems. The reports of committees that have received submissions from the public while examining the problem that the legislation was designed to address, or the legislation itself at a later date, are particularly useful.

5.2.7 Comparative research

Comparative legal research is the examination of the laws of other jurisdictions on the issues under consideration. The aim is to enable a proper evaluation of the approach and experience of other key jurisdictions in addressing the issue. This is particularly useful where other jurisdictions have had their solution in place for a period sufficient for there to be case law and commentary, in the form of judicial pronouncement, parliamentary reviews and reports, law reform agency reports, legal academic research and so forth on its performance, successes and failings. This is valuable in seeking to avoid pitfalls and in tailoring legislative options or solutions that are appropriate for the home jurisdiction of the law reformer. The same process that was used to research the law in the home jurisdiction will be applied to the research in another jurisdiction.

Comparative legal research involves investigating how comparable jurisdictions address a common issue in order to identify reform options. It involves careful consideration of questions of applicability and relevance.

Comparative legal research therefore seeks to investigate how comparable jurisdictions address a common issue in order to identify reform options, and the advantages and disadvantages of each. This involves a critical exercise of judgement, in both the planning of the research and in assessing the results. As regards the planning, it is essential to define the scope of the comparative research, to ensure that only appropriate and useful comparisons for the home jurisdiction are investigated; and that the research results are available within a specified timescale.

It is fundamental to comparative legal research that it should not be approached as simply a way of cutting and pasting a legislative approach used elsewhere without consideration of the local context of both jurisdictions. The aim is not to simply imitate another jurisdiction, but to draw from, and apply as appropriate, experience from elsewhere.

Cybercrime in Jamaica and Nigeria

Consideration of legislation on cybercrime in Jamaica drew on the Council of Europe Convention on Cybercrime. This convention addresses issues such as offences against the confidentiality, integrity and availability of computer data and systems, computer-related offences, content-related offences related to child pornography, and offences related to infringements of copyright and related rights. In the context of Jamaica, however, it was decided that the Cybercrimes Act 2010 would not deal with content-related offences or copyright offences. These were already dealt with in specific legislation addressing these issues; that is, the Child Pornography (Prevention) Act and the Copyright Act. Nigeria's Cybercrimes (Prohibition, Prevention, etc.) Act 2015, by contrast, incorporates these issues into the same legislation.

Legal reforms in other countries, where found useful, must be considered and adapted to suit the local constitutional and legal system, and jurisprudence, as well as the social, cultural and political environments. For example, in several jurisdictions in the USA, sex offenders' registries are open to the public and their contents available online. Serious consideration is required in determining the benefits and challenges of such an approach and whether this would be an appropriate or preferred law reform option for another particular country context.

There is a vast amount of material available online from government ministries, law reform agencies, academia, and the legal and other professional groups, among others, from many jurisdictions.

For many law reformers, particularly in small developing common law states, it may be tempting to seek solutions primarily from jurisdictions such as the United Kingdom, Canada and Australia. However, because of the range of material now available online, it is also possible to research the law in smaller jurisdictions, which may be more appropriate in some cases. Where possible, a search should be made for law reform agency reports from comparable jurisdictions, given the wide networks of law reform agencies and legal information institutes now available.

Naturally, it is often convenient to start looking at large and developed jurisdictions that have a long history of publications of relevant legal material. However, for developing countries, more suitable ideas may be found in the law reform agencies and jurisprudence of developing states.

Naturally, it is often convenient to start by looking at large and developed jurisdictions that have a long history of publications of relevant legal materials, frequently updated by law reform agencies, government departments and parliament. Nonetheless, it is important that law reformers in smaller and medium-sized developing countries do not limit searches because of this. For developing countries, solutions that may be more culturally and situationally appropriate may be found in the law reform agencies and jurisprudence in developing states.

Although primary reliance may be placed on material from the Commonwealth jurisdictions with predominantly common law jurisprudence, the experience of other jurisdictions can be useful. There may be difficulties accessing the law in civil jurisdictions because of practical considerations such as language differences. Nonetheless, it is important to recognise the mixed common law/civil law heritage of such accessible countries as Scotland and South Africa.

Certain Commonwealth countries have civil law traditions and systems in addition to the common law, and this must be taken into consideration when conducting comparative research.

The use of a consultant to carry out relevant comparative research may be of particular value to the law reform agency (see also section 5.4 'Resources for research: consultants and collaboration'). A legal expert, for example from legal academia, could be commissioned to conduct comparative research into a particular issue, and prepare a paper for the agency to consider analysing different approaches from other key jurisdictions and whether or not these would work in the home jurisdiction. The research paper may be published as part of or along with their own consultation document or report.

5.3 Empirical research and the use of other disciplines

Law does not exist in a vacuum. It is part of the fabric of human and community interaction in society. As a result, the law reform researcher may have to have regard to other academic disciplines, particularly the social sciences and empirical research, that seek to ground observation and analysis on data that can inform legal policy. Where possible, and to a greater or lesser extent depending on the issue being addressed, qualitative and quantitative research can assist in obtaining the best or a better picture of the context in which the law operates, of the difficulties with the current law and of the way ahead for reform.

Research outside the discipline of law can be illuminating and provide useful qualitative and quantitative information on which to base reform recommendations.

Empirical studies for these purposes may involve surveys of public opinion on the necessity for new law or reform of the law, or the acquisition and analysis of sociological, demographic or health and medical data. These bring a quantitative element to the examination of the operation and effect of existing law in practice.

A cost–benefit analysis is an example of non-legal information that is often of value.

Commissioning new empirical work of any complexity can be a challenge for law reform agencies, whatever their size. It is frequently expensive, and will often take a considerable time to commission and conduct, which may not fit with the timetable constraints of the project. However, there is, internationally, a very great deal of social science and other empirical research that has been conducted and reported, and it may often be more appropriate to ensure a proper review is undertaken of existing research, rather than to commission new, bespoke research.

Further, it may be possible to work collaboratively with these institutions and with government statistical data resources to prepare useful material for a law reform project.

A particular form of non-legal information that will often be of considerable benefit to law reform projects is the development of cost–benefit analysis, applied to reform proposals. Cost–benefit analysis is dealt with more fully in Chapter 7. It should be noted, however, that many established procedures for implementing cost–benefit analysis require the process to start at the earliest stages of the project.

Behaviour of public bodies and sentencing: Non-legal research in England and Wales and South Africa

When undertaking a wide-ranging project on the law relating to remedies against public bodies, the Law Commission for England and Wales realised that it required insight on the impact of changes in liability on the behaviour of public bodies: whether legal liability led to excessive risk-aversion ('defensive administration') or improved the quality of service provided to the public. It was not possible to commission new empirical research, so a professor of public policy at Bristol University was commissioned to produce a literature review, at moderate cost. The 70-page review covered socio-legal studies, economic approaches, including behavioural economics, public choice theory, decision theory and psychological approaches, and was distilled into a 20-page appendix to the consultation paper.[4]

An empirical quantitative and qualitative study of the sentencing practices of the South African Criminal Courts, with particular emphasis on the Criminal Law Amendment Act 105 of 1997, formed part of the South African Law Reform Commission's review of the sentencing law. The study was undertaken on behalf of the Commission by experts affiliated to the Institute of Criminology at the University of Cape Town. The aims of the study were to determine what sentences were given for various crimes in various regions; the factors that affected those sentences; the impact of the Act investigated on sentencing practices; and to compare sentencing practice with the requirements of the Act. The study informed the research for the Commission's investigation into sentencing law and was published as part of the Commission's research series.[5]

5.4 Resources for research: consultants and collaboration

A law reform agency may possess all the legal or other expertise that may be required for the research project. Commissioners who are experts in the law are usually appointed to carry out the law reform work; in many law reform agencies, supported by Commission legal and research staff. The depth of legal support will depend on the resources available to a law reform agency. If the law reform agency does not have the necessary expertise, consideration may be given to the engagement of consultants or the formation of an advisory group of external experts to advise the law reform agency, in order to provide relevant legal or non-legal expertise for the project in question.

The question to be considered is whether or not the subject matter of research requires or could benefit from external expertise. This involves questions of cost and the availability of consultants or advisory group members. It may also be possible to access technical assistance through regional or international organisations.

Universities and other research institutions can be a good source of potential consultants or advisory group members with academic and research skills and expertise in particular areas, who could be engaged on a full-time or part-time basis for particular projects. Legal practitioners of particular repute and knowledge, as well as retired judges, may also make good consultants or advisory group members.

Consultants may also be practitioners in the relevant field. Other sources of consultants include professional associations and self-regulatory bodies such as bar associations and medical councils; university teaching and research institutions; other government agencies; non-governmental organisations; and international organisations such as the United Nations Educational, Scientific and Cultural Organisation and the United Nations Office on Drugs and Crime.

International assistance: Drugs in Jamaica

Drugs courts were established in Jamaica as a result of the Drugs Court (Treatment and Rehabilitation of Offenders) Act 1999. The process was aided by technical assistance from the Inter-American Drug Abuse Control Commission, an agency of the Organization of American States, which was a source of comparative laws, statistical data and experience, and examples of good practice from other jurisdictions that had previously established drug treatment courts.

Working with academics: The Scottish experience

An example of collaborative working that obtains access for a law reform agency to resources and expertise for research is the memorandum of understanding that was entered into between the Scottish Law Commission and Scotland's university law schools in 2016. The agreement was made to promote law reform in Scotland, by providing a framework for enhanced joint working between the Commission and the legal academic community. It involves university academic staff, post-graduate students and others contributing research to the Commission's law reform projects. The first placement involved an academic from the University of Glasgow School of Law undertaking a comparative research study into selected jurisdictions in order to contribute information and analysis to the Commission's project on the reform of the law on enforcement of securities over land and buildings.

It may also be useful to consider the possibility of collaborative work to obtain the benefit of consultancy-type expertise and additional resources to reduce costs.

5.5 Pre-consultation engagement with stakeholders

One reason for engaging with stakeholders in the field that is the subject matter of the law reform project is so that they can assist with initial research, as discussed above.

There are, however, other reasons. In particular, early engagement with stakeholders can bring considerable benefits in terms of the management of the consultation process to best effect. Lawyers will usually be aware of the existence of the law reform agency, and may well have used or contributed to its work. The same frequently cannot be said for most non-legal stakeholders in the area being examined.

Engaging with stakeholders can assist with legal research, educate both law reform agencies and stakeholders, and raise stakeholder interest and enthusiasm.

It is often the case, therefore, that lay stakeholders in the area of the law under review will not understand law reform. They will not know what the law reform agency is. They will not be clear about its relationship with government. If, however, they understand its record of success in achieving legislative change, they will likely be much more ready to get involved. On the other hand, they will not necessarily understand the limits to law reform. They might, for instance, seek to influence it to take an inappropriately political line. Above all, they will not understand the law reform process, and therefore they will not know how and when to feed in their views and expertise.

On the other side, law reformers will be capable of researching and understanding the law using their own and allied skills. What they will not necessarily understand is the 'feel' of the field. How does the market, or the public service, actually work? How do the different groups of practitioners in the field relate to each other? How do the non-lawyers relate to the lawyers? How do they consume the law? Do they look directly at legislation, or is it filtered through practice and training? What are their pressing day-to-day concerns?

Getting to know the stakeholders early can bring substantial advantages to both sides.

Engaging with stakeholders in advance of public consultation can take many forms. At one end of the spectrum, the law reform agency may feel it is sufficient to write to a relatively small number of stakeholders to convey the necessary information. It is, however, usually worth considering going further than this. In the first instance, it is often desirable for members of the project team to arrange one-to-one meetings with the main organisations in the field. In doing so, law reformers may hear of others that they should also meet.

Even if the project team does not consider that it needs it to generate information, it is often useful to convene a working group or advisory group well before consultation, even if for only a single meeting. It will give the agency the opportunity to explain itself and the process to the stakeholders attending and provide them with a feeling of understanding what will happen and when. This will bring immediate practical benefits in that it allows the stakeholders to plan their contribution to the consultation, which may for instance include organising a conference or seminar during the consultation period or preparing local groups or branches to consider the issue at the right time.

Being a member of an advisory group can confer some status on the individuals concerned, which may also bring benefits to the agency. Even if it was not the motive, bringing together a group of people well versed in the field will always yield some new insight or piece of information. The terms 'working group' or 'advisory group' suggest a small gathering, and that may be the right approach, depending on the project. However, the Law Commission for England and Wales, when undertaking projects, frequently has up to 60 or 70 attendees at advisory group meetings.

It may also be appropriate and useful for the project team to take part in activities that give them direct experience of the field under consideration. Such 'observational consultation' is considered in detail in the next chapter, but it should be noted that it can be undertaken at this earlier stage as well as during the consultation process proper.

5.6 Legal policy: developing the proposals and options

5.6.1 From analysis to proposals and questions

Having completed the initial research and acquired sufficient material to come to a comprehensive view of the area of law within the jurisdiction and in other jurisdictions that have comparable laws, the next step is the analysis of the material and the development of provisional proposals. Research is an organic process and as the material is collected and analysed various possible approaches will often become clear. The analytical review of the material itself will provide suggestions for reform and approaches that have been taken or avoided in other jurisdictions. It is here that judgement, experience and knowledge by the researcher of the community in which the law reform agency is situated will have to be exercised.

The material collected in the research effort must be analysed by reference to the law reform problem.

The point of the analysis is to understand the legal and other dynamics that give rise to what is perceived as the problem that requires law reform attention. Whichever approach to questions or proposals is adopted, it must arise directly out of the analysis and be presented within the narrative in a way that explains why those are the conclusions, or the questions, that the law reform agency thinks address that aspect or problem. The reader should be able to understand why the consultation document is asking the question or making the proposal in relation to the issue or problem under discussion. If there are weaknesses in a proposal, or difficulties in the way that a question has to be posed, those should be set out and discussed. The more honest the presentation of the struggle that the agency is engaged with, for what will almost invariably be difficult questions, the more the reader will understand and be able to engage with the issues.

5.6.2 Questions and proposals

The possible range of first stage documents was covered above. Purely information-providing documents, including scoping reports, do not require consideration of the positive reform proposals. As for those documents, of whatever name, that are intended to form the basis of the consultation, the project team must reach a decision about how open or prescriptive the document's presentation of proposals and questions should be.

Some consultation documents, particularly those produced by government ministries early in the policy formation process, ask questions of a very open and general nature, often proceeding from a fairly thin factual and analytical base. Practice among law reform agencies varies but, as a general tendency, where law reformers can include a stronger and more informed analysis, they will. This in turn tends to close off unsuitable avenues for reform, leaving fewer, but more meaningful, issues open.

Most law reform agency consultation documents contain a mixture of determinate provisional proposals, which the consultee is asked to agree or disagree with, and options, which may be presented neutrally and made the subject of a question. Some may include open questions, although these will tend to be on less fundamental issues. But within that mix, very different emphases are possible. Practice varies among law reform agencies and indeed within a law reform agency in respect of different projects.

Law reform agency consultation documents usually contain a mixture of determinate provisional proposals, which the consultee is asked to agree or disagree with; options, which may be presented neutrally; and open questions.

As a general rule, the Law Commission for England and Wales tends to have the view that the more worked out the provisional proposals are, the more robust and informed the consultation will be. One might see the consultation or working paper as a means of setting up as clear a structure as possible for the purpose of determining whether or not it can withstand consultation. What is left standing at the end is likely to be correct.

The danger with this approach is that it is possible to give the impression that the law reform agency has made up its mind at this stage, which may detract from the quality and vigour of the consultation process.

Australian Law Reform Commission: Questions and proposals

In 2013 to 2014, the Commission undertook an inquiry on equality, capacity and disability in Australian law.[6]

This is an extract from the issues paper summary, listing the questions asked in the relevant chapter.

The National Disability Insurance Scheme

Question 12. What changes, if any, should be made to the *National Disability Insurance Scheme Act 2013* (Cth) and NDIS Rules, or disability services, to ensure people with disability are recognised as equal before the law and able to exercise legal capacity?

Question 13. What changes, if any, should be made to the nominee or child's representative provisions under the *National Disability Insurance Scheme Act 2013* (Cth) or NDIS Rules to ensure people with disability are recognised as equal before the law and able to exercise legal capacity?

Question 14. What changes, if any, should be made to the nominee provisions or appointment processes under the following laws or legal frameworks to ensure they interact effectively:

    a.   the *National Disability Insurance Scheme Act 2013* (Cth) and NDIS Rules;

    b.   social security legislation; and

    c.   state and territory systems for guardians and administrators?

And this is the same section in the discussion paper summary:

5. The National Disability Insurance Scheme

Proposal 5–1. The objects and principles in the *National Disability Insurance Scheme Act 2013* (Cth) should be amended to ensure consistency with the National Decision-Making Principles.

Proposal 5–2. The *National Disability Insurance Scheme Act 2013* (Cth) and NDIS Rules should be amended to include supporter provisions consistent with the Commonwealth decision-making model.

Proposal 5–3. The *National Disability Insurance Scheme Act 2013* (Cth) and NDIS Rules should be amended to include representative provisions consistent with the Commonwealth decision-making model.

Question 5–1. How should the *National Disability Insurance Scheme Act 2013* (Cth) and NDIS Rules be amended to clarify interaction between supporters and representatives appointed in relation to the NDIS, other supporters and representatives, and state and territory appointed decision-makers?

Question 5–2. In what ways should the *National Disability Insurance Scheme Act 2013* (Cth) and NDIS Rules in relation to managing the funding for supports under a participant's plan be amended to:

    a.   maximise the opportunity for participants to manage their own funds, or be provided with support to manage their own funds; and

    b.   clarify the interaction between a person appointed to manage NDIS funds and a state or territory appointed decision-maker?

The Australian Law Reform Commission frequently publishes first an issues paper and then a discussion paper, both of which are subject to consultation. The issues paper will have a much higher preponderance of questions, although some may be bounded, or ask if the consultee agrees with a statement. The discussion paper still has some questions, but has a greater preponderance of proposals, and the questions and proposals are distinguished typographically, whereas in the issues paper, everything is presented as a question.

In South Africa, the Law Reform Commission has adopted a general policy of first compiling an issues paper as a first step to announcing an investigation, to clarify the aim and extent of the investigation and to suggest the options available for solving existing problems within a particular area of the law. The paper is distributed as widely as possible for general information and comment and, where appropriate, may be supplemented by public and/or focused workshops. Responses to an issues paper, coupled with further intensive research, form the basis of preparing a discussion paper. A discussion paper contains essential information on the investigation and the Commission's tentative proposals for reform. In particular, a discussion paper includes a statement of the existing legal position and its deficiencies, a comparative survey and a range of possible solutions. In most cases, the discussion paper also includes a draft bill. Discussion papers are distributed widely and the Commission's preliminary views are usually also explained at public workshops with the aim of gathering informed public comment. Both the issues paper and the discussion paper usually include specific questions to facilitate the public response.

5.6.3 Proposals and questions: some practical issues

On a practical level, it is important to clearly set out the formal questions or proposals that the law reform agency wants the consultees to address. It is often helpful to consultees to set out, in a summary or appendix, the list of questions and proposals (as in the above examples from the Australian Law Reform Commission).

The proposals and questions should also be clearly labelled or numbered – any ambiguity or uncertainty will make the analysis of responses and subsequent work much harder. Law reform

The formal questions or proposals that the consultee must address should be set out clearly in brief, simple sentences.

agencies frequently publish shorter summary documents along with the full consultation document. Despite the effect it will have on the length of the summary document, the proposals and questions should appear in exactly the same words and according to the same numbering scheme as in the full paper. Some consultees will work from the summary rather than the full document, and any divergence between the two will lead to difficulties during the consultation period and for analysis.

It follows that the questions and proposals should, as far as possible, be drafted so that they are grammatically free-standing and do not rely, for their sense, on a cross-reference. The extent to which this can always be accomplished is of course limited. Questions and proposals will inevitably rely on the discussion and detail provided in the full paper. But they should at least be capable of being read and understood, if not fully, on their own. More generally, consultees will spend a lot of time and energy on the law reform agency's proposals and questions. As such, time spent on being sure that the agency's drafting is clear and unambiguous is well spent.

Writing for the public: Everything should be made as simple as possible, but not simpler

Law reformers face a difficult task: how do you explain complicated law to a wide audience, most of whom are not lawyers? This is central to what law reformers do. However, it puts pressure on staff. People who work for law reform agencies have to be not only excellent lawyers but also superb communicators.

Some writing and communication tips are listed below:

Sentence length: keep them short. Most common law lawyers will have read some Lord Denning judgments. While his judgments took this approach to the extreme, generally good writing uses some short sentences, but also varies sentence length within a paragraph.

Be human: do not cut out the human action. When discussing a case, a lawyer will understand the shortest description ('In *A v B*, an action for breach of contract, the claimant was awarded substantial damages'). But most people will need that density to be unpacked. It is therefore important to tell the human story as well as getting the essential law in. Use the active voice rather than passive: 'The judge awarded damages' not 'damages were awarded'.

Use one word when one will do: English lawyers used to be paid by the word, so tended to use two words for a single concept, for example 'will and testament' and 'aid and abet'. Using one word is preferable. Ask what the second word adds to the sense. If one is covered by the other, use the more general one. Further, avoid long-winded prepositions. Therefore, use 'if x happens' not 'in the event of x occurring'; 'about x', not 'in respect of x'.

Notes

1   P M Bakshi, 'Legal Research and Law Reform', (1982) 24 Journal of the Indian Law Institute 391.
2   Particular care should be taken to note the reported status of legislation on this website, as amendments made to Acts may take some time to appear in the version presented.
3   https://www.lawcom.gov.uk/project/year-and-a-day-rule-in-homicide/
4   https://www.lawcom.gov.uk/project/administrative-redress-public-bodies -and-the-citizen/
5   http://salawreform.justice.gov.za/dpapers/dp91.pdf
6   http://www.alrc.gov.au/inquiries/legal-barriers-people-disability

Chapter 6

Consultation

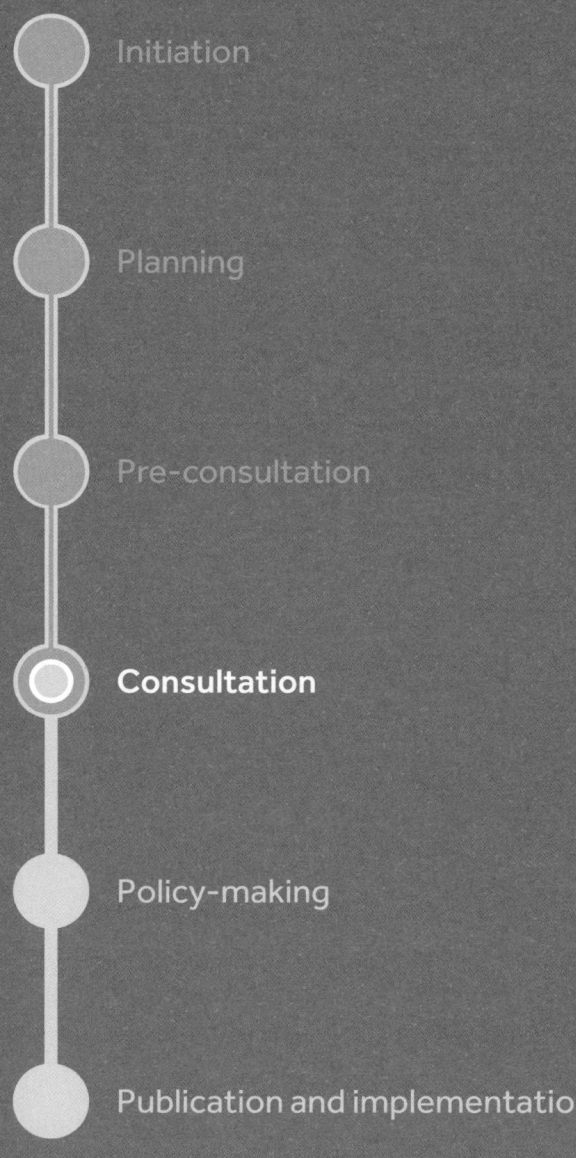

Initiation

Planning

Pre-consultation

Consultation

Policy-making

Publication and implementation

Chapter 6
Consultation

Chapter 6 addresses the role of consultation as a definitive element of law reform. Following a discussion of why consultation is important, the chapter considers different forms of consultation process. It goes on to discuss identification of the audience for consultation and the publication process. The chapter then looks at active consultation – how law reform agencies reach out to the communities with which they aim to engage through advisory groups, meetings and events, and observational consultation and site visits. It underlines the importance of record keeping. It examines the persistent problem of difficult-to-reach interests – how do law reform agencies reach out to those communities that are not organised in such a way as to be readily accessible to the law reformer? Finally, the chapter considers some of the practical issues in relation to written responses, such as time extensions and confidentiality.

Since the inception of modern law reform agencies, consultation has been central to law reform. The other work of law reform agencies may sometimes be performed without consultation, such as some consolidations or reviews of statutes. Occasionally, law reform agencies may perform other functions, such as providing advice to ministers, that do not require consultation. However, law reform agencies' core function of law reform, as it has developed, sees consultation as close to definitional.

6.1 Why consult?

Law reform agencies consult for three principal reasons. First, consultation is good in its own right. Secondly, consultation helps the law reform agency in a practical way to conduct a law reform project. Finally, consultation helps the law reform agency achieve its aims by conferring legitimacy and enhancing its reputation. The account in this chapter focuses primarily on the second of these reasons.

6.1.1 Consultation is a civil right

Consultation is an essential part of law reform. Law reform agencies must consult because consultation is necessary to produce good reforms, people have a right to be consulted, and consultation supports the integrity and reputation of the law reform agency.

People have a right to be consulted. The rule of law itself includes recognition of the importance of participation in decision-making:

> *...a principle of governance in which all persons, institutions and entities, public and private, including the State itself, are accountable to laws that are publicly promulgated, equally enforced and independently adjudicated, and which are consistent with international human rights norms and standards. It requires, as well, measures to ensure adherence to the principles of supremacy of law, equality before the law, accountability to the law, fairness in the application of the law, separation of powers, **participation in decision-making**, legal certainty, avoidance of arbitrariness and **procedural and legal transparency**.[1]*

It is therefore part of the proper law-making procedure in a democracy to provide an opportunity to the people who will be subject to the laws to have a reasonable degree of participation in the making of those laws, over and above their role as electors. As Sachs J said in the South African Constitutional Court:[2]

> *All parties interested in legislation should feel that they have been given a real opportunity to have their say, that they are taken seriously as citizens and that their views matter and will receive due consideration at the moments when they could possibly influence decisions in a meaningful fashion. The objective is both symbolical and practical: the persons concerned must be manifestly shown the respect due to them as concerned citizens, and the legislators must have the benefit of all inputs that will enable them to produce the best possible laws.*

This quotation highlights the link between the normative and the practical, or instrumental, reasons for consultation.

6.1.2 Consultation is essential for the project

At a practical level, good-quality consultation is essential for good-quality law reform. It provides new information and new insights, and brings important strategic benefits.

Consultation provides law reformers with new information. Law reform concerns not just the law in the abstract, but how the law works in the real world. However good the pre-consultation preparation has been, consultation always provides more hard information on how the law works in practice in the relevant field.

Consultation also brings new insights. These may arise because they are informed by practical knowledge of the field. Law reformers, however well informed and skilled, do not have a monopoly on insight. As such, the gleaning of new information and new insights is a key advantage of consultation on a law reform project.

Consultation also brings strategic advantages. By consulting, the law reform agency will become better acquainted with the position of those who support and those who oppose the proposals. The probing of the position of opponents, in particular, will help the law reform agency to understand where some compromise at a later stage will enhance the prospect of implementation. The agency can then make a judgement as to whether, for instance, a compromise on a subsidiary matter is worthwhile for the greater benefit of the implementation of a whole scheme. At the extreme, consultation can effectively become a means of negotiating a compromise or consensus approach that players who are otherwise in conflict can sign up to.

Law reform agencies should never allow themselves to become mere policy fixers. The great benefit of law reform through law reform agencies is that it provides a politically neutral and rational form of legal policy-making. But on the other hand they should seek to understand the dynamics of influence within the field and to accommodate them in an appropriate way.

6.1.3 Consultation is essential for the success of the law reform agency

Good-quality consultation enhances the reputation of the law reform agency and makes it more likely to be effective.

A justified claim to extensive and impartial consultation strengthens the legitimacy of the law reform process. Policy officials, ministers and parliamentarians are more likely to trust the outcome of a law reform process if they can be assured that it is in part the result of such engagement. The relevant policy officials may take a close interest in the agency's consultation process in a specific project. But more generally, the law reform agency will also be judged on the general reputation it has earned for its approach to consultation. Guarding and enhancing this reputation is therefore of high importance.

6.1.4 Limits to consultation

*Most often,
law reform
recommendations
are broadly
consistent with
the results of
the consultation
process.*

Consultation should not determine the final view of the law reform agency. Sometimes, consultation can be negative.

Consultation is not an election. Even if everyone who responds to a consultation process is of one mind about a proposal, it is still incumbent on the law reform agency to consider the proposal on its merits. First, it is a mistake to assume that the results are, necessarily, a true reflection of public opinion on a matter. The sample is, broadly, self-selecting and never weighted to reflect the population. But, secondly, even if it were, consultation, as conducted by law reform agencies, is a public *engagement* process, not a public *determination* process. Law reform agencies consult in order to better perform their public function, not to evade responsibility for it.

Not all consultation is constructive. In extreme cases, the reaction of consultees, or one particularly important consultee, can be so negative that it threatens the whole project. In this, very unusual, situation, a law reform agency may feel the best course is to save future expenditure and effort by terminating the project.

England and Wales: Withdrawing a project on the basis of consultation outcome

In 2008, the Law Commission for England and Wales consulted on a project on the remedies available against public bodies, including the central government. It included proposals to reform both public and private law, in particular proposing a new schema for the liability of public bodies in negligence. The responses on the latter were almost universally negative. The government's response was wholly and implacably opposed. In response, the Commission decided to do no more work on these proposals, and this was announced in a subsequent annual report.

6.2 Consultation processes

*A written
consultation may
be based on a
single, thorough
document or on
multiple documents
at different stages of
the consultation.*

While consultation is always a component of a law reform project, consultation, both written and face to face, can be organised in different ways. Two main patterns have emerged for law reform consultation *documents*. One relies on a single, well worked-through document. The second uses an initial, more open document followed by consultation on a more

British Columbia Law Institute consultations

The British Columbia Law Institute generally identifies key stakeholders representing the various interests affected by the law under study at the beginning of a project. A project committee is established, composed largely of stakeholder representatives. Members of staff carry out research and writing. The committee on the Institute's project on strata property law also includes a representative of the ministry responsible in the provincial government.[3] The committee members assist with identifying the issues that need to be addressed and a work plan is established. The committees usually meet for two hours every month, at least nine or ten times a year. Between meetings, committee members may consult with their stakeholder organisations or clients. Once tentative recommendations are finalised, a consultation process occurs on the standard pattern, based on a consultation paper. The consultation period may last three months, or sometimes longer. Responses are then reviewed by the committee, refined and a final report is prepared.

The committee is seen as critical to ensuring many voices and perspectives are heard. It means that the Institute internalises stakeholder input from the start of the project, as well as seeking external input from a wider group of consultees subsequently.

worked out scheme. Law reform agencies also use consultative techniques such as advisory groups to involve stakeholders early.

The first, and most commonly used, is the straightforward method of publishing a single consultation document and inviting comments during an open consultation period on the basis of that document.

However, law reform agencies have developed other methods. Many law reform agencies consult twice. The Australian Law Reform Commission method – an issues paper followed by a discussion paper, both of which are subject to consultation – is illustrated, in the context of drafting the papers, in the previous chapter. Given the Australian Law Reform Commission's tight timetabling of projects, this approach imposes relatively short consultation periods – less than six weeks, for instance, for the 259-page discussion paper in its Inquiry on Equality, Capacity and Disability in Commonwealth Laws.

This approach, however, has the potential advantage of allowing a deeper engagement with stakeholders. In addition to reacting to a worked-through scheme of reform, as in most one-shot consultation processes, stakeholders are able to engage at an early stage with the shaping of the worked-through scheme.

Consultation should be public.

Another way of bringing stakeholders in earlier is to use working groups or advisory groups to help shape the project. They may become part of the drafting process of a single consultation paper. Such groups will meet a number of times, and may be asked to comment on early research memoranda and chapters of the consultation document as they are drafted.

This use of advisory or working groups and committees for substantive input before public consultation is to be contrasted with the use of advisory groups as a preparation for public consultation, as discussed in the previous chapter. In the former, the group is an inherent part of the consultation process. In the latter, it is, largely, a part of the process of preparation for consultation.

6.3 Audiences

Consultation requires careful consideration of the audience that it seeks to reach and involve. This involves a balance between tailoring a consultation process to a pre-selected audience and allowing for general public engagement.

As regards the first, it would defeat the purpose of consultation if the audience is exclusively selected. Consultation, except in extreme circumstances, should be public, in that any member of the public should be able to take part, should they so choose. It is often helpful to emphasise that responses are welcome from any source, not only those approached by the law reformers. Too many potential consultees suppose that a response from them would not be welcome if they have not been approached by law reformers. In addition, it may be helpful to emphasise that responses to some or any question are welcome; it is not necessary to respond to every question asked.

However, in practice, a law reform agency will look primarily at those most closely involved in the field under consideration. The purpose of consultation is to ensure that the law is relevant for its intended objective, and so those most closely affected will be more likely to produce the key consultation responses. The law reform agency should therefore consider who the primary targets of consultation are and ensure that the process works to address them.

Key potential consultees should be selected carefully.

The audience for a technical, 'lawyers' law' project will be very different from that for a wide-ranging regulatory project or a project on criminal law. The difference in audience will determine what documents are produced and the style in which they are written.

It is important not to draw the line too narrowly however. Understanding the full range of stakeholders who may be concerned with the law covered by a project requires imagination and care. This question may have already been addressed by the start of the consultation period if a committee such as the type used by the British Columbia Law Institute or an advisory group, as discussed in the previous chapter, has been set up. If not, it will certainly arise when a list or lists of recipients for documents is drawn up at the commencement of the consultation process.

The nature of the audience will affect the type and style of documents produced.

Drawing up such lists is a key part of targeting consultation. It will often be helpful to ask the policy official responsible in the relevant government department for their list of stakeholders or contacts. General legal stakeholders, with whom the law reform agency will have an ongoing relationship, such as bar associations and law societies, may help. They will often have lists not only of legal stakeholders, but also of 'client' organisations in particular fields. It is also important to ask those who the project team do know are involved: they may be able to suggest who else the team should contact. It is advisable therefore to think laterally. For example, if the agency is looking at a housing or landlord and tenant question, the army, which houses soldiers, may be interested; or it may be worth consulting hoteliers, who provide services that may have to be distinguished from the legal regime that is the subject matter of the project. Even if an agency's work on social services deliberately excludes healthcare, it will need to talk to healthcare professionals about the border between the two and how changes in social services might affect the delivery of healthcare. That some relevant stakeholders will be left off the list is almost inevitable, and can be handled with an apology and belated inclusion.

6.4 Publication: getting the word out

Most law reform agencies publish lengthy consultation documents to commence the public consultation period or periods. Increasingly, supporting documents are also used. These may include summaries and papers or leaflets aimed at particular constituencies of consultees.

6.4.1 Print and web publication

Should law reform agencies publish online only, or also in print?

Consultation documents should be shared with stakeholders and the public at large. Publication in print or on the web, in the press or on social media, or via professional networks will be appropriate for different issues and different stakeholders.

Nearly all law reform agencies maintain a web presence and use their website to publish documents online. Producing only a print version is hardly an option these days. It is possible for a consultation document to appear only online. Nonetheless, most law reform agencies still print at least a relatively small number of hard copies for distribution to stakeholders.

Experience suggests that, contrary to what might be expected given the ubiquity of the internet, most consultees, including those in large and professional organisations, still use hard copies when composing their responses. Providing a document only, or mainly, on the internet is very much cheaper for the law reform agency. If the agency does not print documents, a well-resourced organisation will print its own from the online files. However, smaller organisations, charities and individuals may not be able to print documents, and the lack of a hard copy may disadvantage them. It is for each law reform agency, in relation to each project, to find the appropriate balance.

The law reform agency's database of stakeholders will therefore receive either a hard copy, with a letter inviting a response, or an email with a link to the document on the agency's website, or a mixture of the two.

6.4.2 Press and social media

At the point of publication, press interest is particularly welcome to promote the existence of the project to potential consultees.

Some larger law reform agencies may employ communications professionals, but most will not, in which case the task of press relations will fall to the project team or to the chief executive of the agency.

As with other major stages, the law reform agency will prepare and distribute to journalists a press/media release. This guide is not the place to provide wide-ranging advice on press relations in general, or the preparation of press/media releases in particular. General training and advisory materials on press relations will be useful to law reform agencies.

It may be helpful, however, to mention two related aspects of press relations relating to law reform.

The first is that lawyers and law reformers can risk overestimating general public interest in the topic of law reform. At least in larger countries, where there is more competition, it is very difficult to get the main popular newspapers or television and radio news programmes to take an item that involves any degree of legal complexity. While some law reform subjects, such as many criminal issues, certainly do interest mainstream news outlets, other subjects will struggle to get coverage, and it is often much better to target specialist outlets. Those may be specialist legal outlets. Just as important, if not more so, are specialist outlets aimed at the professional audience or audiences in the relevant field. In smaller jurisdictions, it may be easier to secure broader media interest.

The second and related point is that even the specialist press will want a simple story. Reality is rarely simple enough, and lawyers tend to focus on details and accuracy. When interesting a news outlet in a story, the lawyer has to let go of qualifications and nuance, while retaining a broadly accurate account.

Whether it is useful to hold a press conference to launch a publication will depend on the likely interest in the project, the press expertise of the agency and the receptiveness of the press in that jurisdiction. However, it will rarely be the case that it will be advisable for an agency to adopt a general practice of holding a press conference.

Some law reform agencies have a presence on social media such as Twitter and Facebook. These allow the agency to disseminate information directly to the public. The Law Commission for England and Wales has more than 12,000 followers on Twitter, for instance. It is also possible for a law reform agency to establish a Twitter feed and Facebook page dedicated to a particular project. These avenues may prove a useful way of keeping stakeholders and consultees in touch with a project as it develops. As yet, they have not been used as a conduit for responses.

6.4.3 Networks

Media publicity does not exhaust the ways in which stakeholders can be reached. A particularly important resource is stakeholders' own networks.

The agency will have undertaken pre-consultation preparatory engagement with stakeholders or used small working/advisory groups at an earlier stage. This is the opportunity to discuss with stakeholders how best to engage their own networks.

Nearly all of the organisations with which law reform agencies engage will be located within networks. Some will be membership bodies with local branches. Charities and voluntary organisations will be members of national and often regional or global umbrella bodies. Companies will be members of trade associations, and professionals will have both professional and subject matter-related representative bodies. Such networks usually have methods of regular communication with their members, and could be approached to include information about a relevant consultation in a newsletter or regular email. It is often more effective for that explanation to come from a trusted, known network, rather than from a law reform agency of which the recipient may have only limited knowledge.

6.5 Active consultation

Law reform agencies actively seek engagement with stakeholders. For example, this can be done through advisory/working groups.

There may once have been a time when law reform agencies published consultation documents and then passively waited for responses to arrive. That is generally no longer the case. Formal written responses from organisations and individuals remain central to law reform agency consultation. But the consultation period or periods are also used much more now as an opportunity to actively engage with stakeholder communities in a dialogue on the law reform agency's proposals and alternatives to them. This section considers some of the methods that may be used.

6.5.1 Advisory/working groups

There are a number of distinct roles that advisory groups/working groups/committees can play during consultation.

The use of advisory groups in the pre-consultation process was discussed above (see Chapter 5). At that point, their function is primarily to prepare the stakeholder community for consultation. As consultation proceeds, their function will adapt. They can be used as forums for discussion on the substance of the issues. This can both act as a direct input into the law reform agency's thinking, and help to inform the

Taxis in England and Wales: A technical legal issue within a regulatory project

The Law Commission for England and Wales's 2011 to 2014 project on the law relating to taxis and private hire vehicles was a broad regulatory law project covering all aspects of the regulation of this market. A key element of the existing regulatory regime is the undefined legal concept, introduced in nineteenth century legislation, of 'plying for hire'. The concept was originally conceived for one purpose (the licensing of taxis and the making of 'plying for hire' a criminal offence for others), but now also forms the essential legal border between what taxis and (pre-booked) private hire cars could do. The case law relating to what 'plying for hire' means is considerable, complicated and difficult to understand. The Law Commission convened, during the course of the consultation period, an 'expert panel on plying for hire' to consider the issue. It consisted of lawyers, some nominated by interested groups such as enforcement officers and trade unions representing taxi drivers, other senior barristers and solicitors in private practice. It crafted a new approach to the legal definition of both taxi and private hire operations that does not rely on the concept of 'plying for hire'.

individual stakeholder members' own subsequent written responses. In addition, such group meetings can be useful if held towards the end of the consultation period, in order to feed back some of the messages that the law reform agency has heard in other ways.

Where a stakeholder working group has been used as a way of integrating stakeholder concerns at an early stage, as for instance in the British Columbia examples set out above, it will continue to perform that function during and after the consultation period. However, it is inevitable that the focus shifts somewhat from internalised consultation structures to the public exercise.

In addition to the uses of working groups or committees already discussed, there may be a role within a broader public consultation for a small, specialist working group to consider a particular, distinct issue.

6.6 Meetings, events and observational consultation

6.6.1 The format of meetings and events

Meetings and events are central to consultation as active dialogue. The format of meetings and events can range in size and formality. There is often tension between the giving

Active dialogue requires meetings. These can vary in size, formality, the balance between giving and receiving information, openness and hosting arrangements.

and receiving of information, which should be considered in determining the right format or formats for particular meetings and events.

In all cases, the law reform agency is concerned with both providing and receiving information and understandings from stakeholders. In the first instance, the agency must explain both what it is provisionally asking or proposing and why. At one level, there is value in simply getting such information out to stakeholders. It will inform stakeholders' own internal conversations, the result of which will be a better response at a later point.

However, there is also considerable benefit to be gained from engaging in a dialogue with stakeholders, a process that puts at least as much emphasis on the law reform agency receiving information and understandings from stakeholders.

The balance between these two features will be different depending on the nature of the event. A formal presentation at a large conference will be very useful in disseminating information to a wide range of individuals, but it will provide very limited opportunity for genuine dialogue. Such opportunities can be enhanced if the conference programme includes workshop or breakout sessions with small groups of attendees, in sessions led by a member of the project team or the advisory/working group. However, doing so where a number of such sessions must be held at the same time naturally poses a challenge to the resources of the project team.

A seminar provides a more balanced environment, allowing for both information dissemination and dialogue. Such events, modelled on academic, pedagogic or research seminars, are usually confined to fewer than 20 or 25 participants. Ideally, participants sit around the same table, rather than facing the presenter in theatre style.

Seminars not only allow the law reform agency to give a full presentation of the consultation proposals and questions, but also allow plenty of time for discussion. Sometimes, discussion can be enhanced by having an individual outside the law reform agency taking on the role of discussant. The idea is that the discussant gives an immediate reaction to the agency's presentation as a way of encouraging participation. This approach is more likely to work if the discussant is critical of some aspects of the agency's approach.

The word 'seminar' is associated with universities and high levels of expertise. As such, it may be off-putting for some stakeholders. Much the same format can be labelled a 'workshop' or 'forum'.

At the other end of the scale from a large conference is a meeting of members of the project team with representatives of a single stakeholder organisation or a small number of stakeholders. This format is the opposite of a conference. As regards disseminating information from the agency, it is very limited in scope. On the other hand, it may provide a great deal of scope for dialogue. It is also much easier to organise than the other types of event.

6.6.2 How public is the meeting or event?

Whatever its format, it is important for there to be a clear understanding as to the extent to which what is said at an event is to be considered public. It should always be made clear at the outset by a clear statement from the chair what the status of the meeting or event is.

There are three main approaches: the meeting or event may be public, it may be held under the Chatham House Rule or it may be confidential. Most conferences will be public and some may be streamed on the internet or recorded for later dissemination. Other events will vary. Some will be fully public. Some will be held under the Chatham House Rule. This rule provides that the results of the event can be made public, but individual contributions should not be attributed to identified speakers. Finally, some may be confidential.

People may be more willing to speak frankly if a meeting or event is confidential or held under the Chatham House Rule, and that can be valuable. However, these contributions will be of less use to the law reform agency than a response that can be quoted and attributed to a named participant. Secrecy can also give rise to unjustified suspicions among those who were not involved, particularly if the issue is one occasioning a high degree of controversy and/or there is limited trust in the project among some stakeholders.

6.6.3 Whose event?

It can be easier, cheaper and more effective for law reform agencies to use other organisations to set up events and meetings. It is, however, critical that the basis upon which the law reform agency is taking part is made clear to avoid any suggestion that the agency is thereby associating itself with the views of the organisation that is responsible for the event.

Events of any size, such as seminars and conferences, take significant resources to organise. Doing so can be a challenge in terms of both budget and staff time. Accordingly, law reform agencies may wish to consider approaching other organisations that may hold events and be willing to extend an invitation to the agency to speak at such an event. This may be an event that is already planned, to which the organisation would like to add the subject matter of the agency's project. Alternatively, if the issue is important to the organisation, they may wish to hold a specific event.

The way in which such events are presented to the public is important. If it is badged as a law reform agency event, but is paid for by a stakeholder organisation, there may be a danger that the law reform agency could be seen to be prejudiced by the relationship.

Sometimes law reform agencies have accepted sponsorship for an official event such as the launch of a project. This may be uncontroversial if the sponsor is a government department, an aid agency or a legal publisher. But if the sponsor is a stakeholder that is likely to take a particular line in relation to the subject matter of the project, or a law firm that preponderantly represents one interest, then questions as to propriety and conflict of interest may arise.

The position is quite different when the event is clearly owned by the stakeholder group, and the law reform agency is appearing as an invited guest to secure the views of that stakeholder or those who attend the event. But for such an approach to escape criticism, the law reform agency must also make it clear that it is open to similar invitations from other groups. The agency will also have to ensure that it does what it can to reach groups that are not organised in a way that allows them to extend such invitations to the agency (see section 6.8 'Difficult-to-reach consultees').

The advantage of a law reform agency organising its own events is that the agency controls the form of the event (conference, seminar, etc.), the content of the event and who is invited. In this way, it can ensure the appropriate balance between interests and, where relevant, an appropriate geographical spread. The law reform agency can also be sure to schedule the events for the timetabled consultation period. In addition, there may be no guarantee that invitations from other organisations, at least in any number, will be forthcoming. So organising its own events can be safer for the agency.

There are countervailing advantages of a consultation strategy that relies on accepting invitations. Because the stakeholder body is organising and paying for the event, it is possible for the project team to reach many more stakeholders. There may also be advantages in going out to meet stakeholders where they are, in sentiment as well as in physical location, such as at a local branch meeting or an organisation's annual conference, rather than trying to bring the stakeholders to the law reform agency.

The difficulty of scheduling events can be significantly mitigated by appropriate pre-consultation engagement with stakeholders. At an early stage, the law reform agency can discuss what events the stakeholders have already planned in the consultation period, and the stakeholders can consider whether or not they wish to arrange a special event for consultation purposes.

It is also not necessary to be too prescriptive about the timing of events. Sometimes, there may be a genuine reason for a high degree of confidentiality. But, otherwise, it is unlikely to harm the process if, at events held before the official start of consultation, the law reform agency, with appropriate warnings, gives an indication of how its thinking is progressing. Likewise, while events held a significant time after the close of consultation will be useful to only a limited extent, they may still be useful for some time.

The choice is not a binary one, however. Even a law reform agency that relies largely on accepting invitations from stakeholders will, nonetheless, be likely to organise a small number of events to address specific questions that might not otherwise arise or to otherwise plug a gap in the range of invitations.

England and Wales: Tenure reform invitations accepted

In its interim report on the project on the reform of tenure for short-term renting, called Renting Homes, the Law Commission for England and Wales published a list of 72 events attended by members of the project team.[4] There were two consultation periods on different aspects of the project, from March to July 2002 and from August to November 2002. The first of the listed events was in February 2002 and the last was in September 2003, although most were concentrated in the consultation periods.

As an example, the following is an extract from the list:

Date	Organisation	Event
23 February	TPAS Nottingham	RSL tenants' conference
20 March	Small Landlords Association London	Meeting
22 March	Social Landlords Crime & Nuisance Group Coventry	Committee meeting
26 March	Association of Law Teachers London	Conference presentation
5 April	Socio-Legal Studies Association Aberystwyth	Conference presentation
18 April	Social Landlords Crime and Nuisance Group Birmingham	Annual Conference
25 April	North East Housing Law Practitioners Association Newcastle	Meeting
9 May	Housing Law Practitioners Association London	Executive Committee meeting
15 May	Socio-Legal Studies Association/Society of Public Teachers of Law London	Academic seminar
15 May	Housing Law Practitioners Association London	General meeting
20 May	Welsh Assembly/Welsh National Housing Federation	Conference
22 May	Essex Citizens Advice Bureau Witham	Housing Policy meeting
27 May	Law Society London	Housing Law Committee meeting
28 May	London School of Economics London	MSc Housing Alumni meeting
5 June	Local Government Association London	Executive meeting

England and Wales: Tenure reform invitations accepted (cont.)

Date	Organisation	Event
7 June	Rent Assessment Panel Birmingham	Meeting
12 June	Chartered Institute of Housing Harrogate	Annual Conference
13 June	National Union of Students London	Meeting
13 June	Bolton Council Bolton	Housing special interest group meeting
18 June	Law Centres Federation London	Seminar
18 June	Tenant Participation Advisory Service Birmingham	Anti-social behaviour Conference
19 June	Brighton Council Brighton	Private Sector Forum meeting

6.6.4 Observational consultation and site visits

Some law reform agencies have taken engagement with stakeholders a stage further. In some projects, it is important for the project team to get a 'feel' for the field or some particular issue causing concern. It is equally important to keep the significance of what members of staff witness in proportion.

This will not be relevant in the more technical legal fields, where a real understanding of the issues can be readily achieved by reading and understanding the legal texts. However, in projects concerned with regulating activities or markets, for instance, it can be helpful to gain insights from observing events or by going on site visits.

Observational consultation of this type can be very helpful in giving members of the project team an inside understanding of how and at what points both the current law and any proposals for reform may come under pressure. There is a concomitant danger that such experience can be *too* vivid, and can therefore mislead the team as to the significance of what they have seen versus other considerations. In the examples in the box below, the late night economy situation was used as an argument to abolish the distinction between taxi cabs and private hire vehicles (both of which are safe cars driven by drivers with criminal record checks) and concentrate on policing 'touts'. Although it floated some half-way house proposals, the Commission eventually recommended

Law reform agency staff can benefit from seeing or experiencing issues and places first hand. However, care must be taken to give appropriate weight to what is seen and experienced.

Observational consultation in South Africa and England and Wales

South Africa

During the course of the South African Law Reform Commission's project on sexual offences and adult prostitution, researchers undertook police-guided and facilitated site visits to a safe-house, brothels, and areas of pimping and street prostitution. Engagements facilitated by non-governmental organisations were also conducted at neutral sites in different provinces with adult prostitutes as part of the public participation process following publication of the Commission's discussion paper for this investigation. Because of the sensitive nature of certain investigations and the risk of harm to interviewees, one-on-one confidential or anonymous interviews were conducted with current or existing prostitutes, ex-brothel keepers and victims of stalking for the purposes of the Commission's investigation into stalking.[5]

England and Wales

The Law Commission for England and Wales undertook a project on the regulation of taxi cabs and private hire vehicles. A particularly intense set of regulatory issues related to the 'late night economy' arose. In certain, often quite small parts of British cities late at night at weekends, as pubs and clubs close, taxi cabs and private hire vehicles become the primary way of transporting large numbers of young people home, many of whom are under the influence of alcohol. At such times, the legal distinctions between taxi cabs (which can be hailed on the street) and private hire cars (which must be booked) and completely illegal vehicles ('touts') come under extreme pressure. There are also critical threats to public order. To understand the issues, members of the team accompanied licensing enforcement officers on operations in London and Liverpool, which included accompanying officers undertaking undercover operations to test the legality of the conduct of private hire drivers. They also accompanied police officers on a similar operation against 'touts' in London.[6]

The same Commission's joint project with the Scottish Law Commission on the law relating to railway level crossings encountered serious problems with its proposals in relation to regulating tram level crossings. The relevant association invited the commissioner and team manager to inspect the layout of the tram system in Sheffield, which they did from a private tram that was able to stop and allow the team to inspect particular features of the system. The team members were also asked to drive the tram on a training track to show the vehicle's capability to undertake an emergency stop. In the same project, team members also conducted a number of site visits to dangerous level crossings with railway officials.[7]

retaining the distinction for other good regulatory reasons. In respect of the tram example, however, the Commission completely changed its proposals to wholly exclude trams.

6.7 Record keeping

Appropriate record keeping of meetings and events is crucial. This applies to meetings of committees and working groups, of

Australian Law Reform Commission: Noting of advisory groups

From the chapter 'Strategic and Project Planning' in *The Promise of Law Reform* by Anne Rees (edited by Opeskin and Weisbrot):

> *Advisory committee meetings are vital to finalising questions, proposals or recommendations. Although there may be consensus on some matters, others will be more controversial and may be opposed by some of the committee. Noting and understanding this range of views is important to the team and to the process of transparency and it underscores the value of effective minute taking. With meetings that may run for up to three hours, minute taking becomes one of the necessary evils of the inquiry process. Staff usually operate in relay pairs and write up the minutes between them.*

whatever nature and stage of the project, and to consultation events. However, what is appropriate may vary.

Full minutes, circulated to members and corrected and accepted at a subsequent meeting, may be essential where the purpose of a committee meeting, or commissioners' or board meeting, is to make formal decisions on behalf of the agency.

It may not be necessary, and indeed may be unhelpful, to try to record what happened at a consultation event. First, creating a full record of this sort is resource intensive. It means that at least two members of staff must be present, one to present and conduct the meeting and the other to take notes. Secondly, writing up effective minutes involves editing and structuring the normal flow of a meeting, and that can take considerable time. To produce good-quality minutes of such a meeting will take some hours back at the office. It is nowadays technically possible to cheaply and easily digitally record a meeting and to store the recording in an accessible way. But there are few purposes efficiently served by listening to the whole of a two-hour meeting, with its repetitions, irrelevancies, silences and interruptions.

Some form of record keeping is always needed, but the appropriate type varies. The production of quality minutes for a meeting takes some hours.

An alternative is for the person presenting and conducting the meeting to complete a short form outlining the nature of the event and providing a few bullet points of further information. A middle ground is used by the Victorian Law Reform Commission, which provides more information than the short form. Comprehensive hand-written notes are taken during the consultation. These are then confirmed as accurate by the participants; the notes then stand as the record but are not published.

Law Commission for England and Wales: Consultation meeting record form

The form below is an example of the meeting and event forms used by some teams at the Law Commission for England and Wales. The form is designed to be completed quickly and easily. It may be filled in as the team member conducting the meeting travels back from the meeting or first thing the following day. The bullet points in most cases will be one or two sentences long.

MEETING RECORD FORM			
[NAME OF PROJECT]			
Subject *(if not the project as a whole)*:			
Date	Meeting organiser	Type of meeting	Number of participants
Nature of participants *(professional, user, lawyer, etc)*:			
Key points *(guidance: 4 to 8 bullet points)*			
• • • • • • • •			
Team member:			

6.8 Difficult-to-reach consultees

Not all potential consultees have representative organisations to speak for them. It is important, when taking into account the views of organised stakeholder groups, that law reform agencies do not miss the contribution of those without representative organisations.

Efforts must be made to reach potential consultees who do not have organised representation. This can require imaginative efforts.

Law reform agencies are in general largely reliant for responses on organised stakeholder groups, including legal professional groups, and academics.

This works well when all major interests are properly represented by effective, professional stakeholder groups. That is, however, frequently not the case. The result is that, unless compensatory steps are taken, the responses to a consultation may be skewed in favour of the well-resourced stakeholder.

Human genetics information and the Australian Law Reform Commission

In its inquiry on the protection of human genetic information (a joint inquiry with the Australian Health Ethics Committee), the Australian Law Reform Commission recognised that widespread public consultation would be a key feature. The agency organised a series of well-publicised (and generally well-attended) public meetings in 15 major cities and towns all over Australia. This was in addition to 185 separate stakeholder meetings, plus a number of conferences and overseas meetings. The Commission also experimented with the use of 45,000 free postcards, made available in public places, such as cafes, in an attempt to reach people who would not otherwise have been aware of the inquiry.

The inquiry received a total of 316 written submissions as a result (to both the issues paper and the discussion paper) and had to extend the consultation period in light of the interest generated.[8]

In some consultations, the missing consultees are the general public. In many projects, this is not necessarily a significant problem. For example, in a technical project on conveying real property, if both sides of the conveyancing transaction are adequately represented, then it is difficult to see what a distinctive 'public' voice would add.

Reaching rural people in Tanzania and South Africa

Tanzania is a large country with a preponderantly rural population (68 per cent). As it is a relatively low-income developing country, there are comparatively few representative or interest groups speaking for the mass of the rural population on legal issues. The Law Reform Commission is based in Dar es Salaam. In order to gauge opinion in rural areas on appropriate projects, the project team travels into the countryside in a Commission vehicle, carrying all of the relevant consultation materials. The aim is to conduct open public meetings in rural towns and villages in relation to a project. The team may spend several weeks on the road in this way. The result is a 'safari report', the aim of which is to feed the views of rural people into the law reform process.

In its project on *ukuthwala* (the forced marriage or sale of young girls into marriages with adult men), the South African Law Reform Commission presented a number of consultative workshops in rural areas to facilitate public comment on the Commission's discussion paper on this issue.[9] The discussion paper published for public comment contained a proposed draft bill reflecting the Commission's preliminary recommendations. The draft bill was translated into several different indigenous languages to make the consultation process as accessible as possible. Public workshops, presented countrywide to facilitate responses to the discussion paper, were also presented in the different indigenous languages spoken in the different provinces to ensure a true understanding of the Commission's views by and to encourage the participation of the indigenous population.

However, in many broader, less technical projects, the views of the public in general may well be of great significance to the direction of law reform.

At other times, law reform agencies have used opinion polling in appropriate projects. Polling can be expensive and the response to a simple polling question can be crude, but it may provide an avenue to explore popular feeling where there are no other options available.

However, there may be other, more imaginative ways to reach the people. Going out to the people is an essential component of consultation in many jurisdictions.

In some projects, the project team may be aware that a particular, clearly interested group is not represented.

When seeking the input of specific populations, it is important to facilitate their ability to participate. Considerations range from the physical accessibility of the premises to public transportation, including reimbursement of transport costs, using the connections of local community groups to reach the target community. Prior to commencing a consultation event, it may even be necessary to ensure that food is provided for those who have not eaten. Most importantly, timeline planning may need to accommodate additional time for locating participants and gaining their trust, and ensuring appropriate follow-up so that participants feel that their opinions and ideas have been heard and considered.

Private tenants: The Law Commission for England and Wales

During the Law Commission for England and Wales project Renting Homes, on renting tenure reform, it became apparent to the project team that a particular category of tenants was unrepresented. Tenants of local authorities and housing associations were well represented by a number of bodies, local and national. Private tenants on pre-1989 Rent Act tenancies, who had security of tenure, were also represented, by a number of active local associations. However, most private tenants with more modern tenancies, with little security of tenure, did not identify with each other as an interest group, and their tenancies were often transitory.

The project accordingly engaged an experienced tenant participation consultancy to undertake a series of focus groups with these private tenants. The focus groups were made up of 10 to 12 tenants. The presenter from the consultancy was provided with a brief, which included questions for discussion. Afterwards, the consultancy submitted a report on the results of the focus group exercise.

6.9 Written responses

Written responses, formally submitted usually at the close of the consultation period, remain a key product of consultation. General issues arise in relation to the form of responses, how strictly time limits for reception of responses should be enforced and whether responses should be publicly available.

6.9.1 The form of responses

Many law reform agencies use online questionnaires for responses, although responses in hard copy are also received. The use of software with online questionnaires can make the analysis of responses quicker and more efficient. Some agencies publish hard copy booklets for responses. Even if separate documents generated by the consultee are used, the law reform agency may ask for them to be submitted in electronic form as well as, or instead of, hard copy, again to assist with the analysis.

6.9.2 The timing of responses

Written responses should be received before the end of the consultation period. As discussed in Chapter 5, advisory groups brought together before consultation starts can be a way of disseminating information about the timetable for the project, including the end of the consultation period. A law reform agency may have a continuing relationship with regular consultees, such as a law society, and can forewarn them of upcoming consultations.

It is nonetheless frequently the case that a significant number of responses to a consultation are received shortly after the deadline for responses. If a response is a week late at the end of a three-month consultation period, the law reform agency is unlikely to be prejudiced and will accept it. But what of significantly late consultation responses? Law reform agencies are frequently asked for extensions of time by stakeholders.

In some cases, a general extension of the time limit may be warranted. This could be because new issues have emerged during the course of the consultation process that require further consideration from stakeholders. Equally, allowing extra time may provide the law reform agency with a way of

Written responses are an important product of consultation. They may be electronic or hard copy. Care is needed in deciding about their availability to the public.

Wildlife law: Athletes and fishermen

In 2012, the Law Commission for England and Wales extended the consultation period for a large-scale project on wildlife law, first in response to representations from stakeholders concerned that the Olympic Games, which were held in London that year, would reduce the time available. Secondly, while the consultation paper sought to limit the marine extent of the project to territorial waters, it asked a question about this time issue. The issue of whether the project should extend to the 200-mile 'exclusive economic zone' also became a live one during consultation, and the deadline was further extended to allow the sea fishing industry to make representations.

accommodating critics: doing so may divert criticism and mean that the likelihood of a more consensual outcome is increased.

Law reform agencies will have different attitudes towards requests for late submission of responses from individual stakeholders. If the timetable for the project is very tight, it may be impossible to accommodate an extension. In general, law reform agencies will want to be able to extend time to get the benefit of an additional response. The law reform agency may need to ensure that there is a clear message as to how much extra time it is likely to allow stakeholders from one project to the next.

The Victorian Law Reform Commission encourages submissions before or early in the consultation period. This has the additional benefit of enabling issues raised in submissions to be progressively consulted upon.

6.9.3 The public availability of responses

The law reform agency should make express provision for whether responses should be considered public documents or not.

In some jurisdictions, the extent to which responses should be made public will be influenced by freedom of information legislation. It may be that the law reform agency cannot impose a general confidentiality rule, even if it wanted to, because responses would be subject to freedom of information requests. A law reform agency may also be covered by government policies in relation to publication or inspection on request of responses to consultations.

In general, most law reform agencies would consider that it is good practice for responses to be publicly available, at least on request. Law reform is a form of public policy formulation and will generally benefit from transparency. On the other hand, agencies will also seek to preserve confidentiality or anonymity upon request in appropriate cases.

Whatever the policy, it should be publicly set out in the consultation document to which the response is made.

The analysis of responses is the key step linking the consultation exercise with the final policy-making process, and to that the next chapter turns.

Status of submissions

The South African Law Reform Commission indicates in all its research papers published for public comment that the Commission will assume that unless comments or representations are marked 'confidential', respondents grant the Commission permission to quote from their comments and to refer to respondents by name. Respondents should further be aware that the Commission may, under the terms of the Promotion of Access to Information Act 2 of 2000, be required to release information contained in representations or comments submitted to the Commission.

The New South Wales Law Reform Commission operates a two-stage consultation process, with question papers and consultation papers. The following is the text that appears in the Commission's question and consultation papers, clearly setting out the Commission's policy:

> We generally publish submissions on our website and refer to them in our publications.

> We will normally publish your submission unless you request confidentiality for all or part of the document (see our Privacy and Information Management Policy for further details). Please let us know if you do not want us to publish your submission, or if you want us to treat all or part of it as confidential.

> We will endeavour to respect your request, but the law provides some cases where we are required or authorised to disclose information. In particular we may be required to disclose your information under the Government Information (Public Access) Act 2009 (NSW).

> In other words, we will do our best to keep your information confidential, but we cannot promise to do so, and sometimes the law or the public interest says we must disclose your information to someone else.

The Commission's privacy and information management policy is published on its website, and makes clear that the name of the person submitting the response will be made public, but not their personal address, telephone number or other personal information.[10]

Notes

1   Definition from United Nations Security Council 2006, paragraph 6 (emphasis added).
2   *Doctors for Life International v The Speaker of National Assembly* 2006 (12) BCLR 1399 (CC). For a useful commentary, see Czapanskiy and Manjoo 2008.
3   http://www.bcli.org/project/strata-property-law-phase-two. Strata property is a statutory form of property holding in which individuals own an interest in their own home and are members of a strata corporation that owns common parts and has obligations in relation to maintenance, etc.
4   http://www.lawcom.gov.uk/wp-content/uploads/2015/03/lc284_Renting_Homes.pdf
5   http://salawreform.justice.gov.za/reports/r-pr107-SXO-AdultProstitution-2017-Sum.pdf
6   https://www.lawcom.gov.uk/project/taxi-and-private-hire-services/
7   https://www.lawcom.gov.uk/project/level-crossings/
8   http://www.alrc.gov.au/publications/1-introduction-inquiry/community-consultation-processes
9   http://www.justice.gov.za/salrc/dpapers/dp132-UkuthwalaRevised.pdf
10 http://www.lawreform.justice.nsw.gov.au/Documents/Publications/Consultation-Papers/CP17.pdf;   http://www.lawreform.justice.nsw.gov.au/Pages/lrc/lrc_policytableddoc/LRC_policydoc/lrc_impp.aspx

Chapter 7

Policy-making

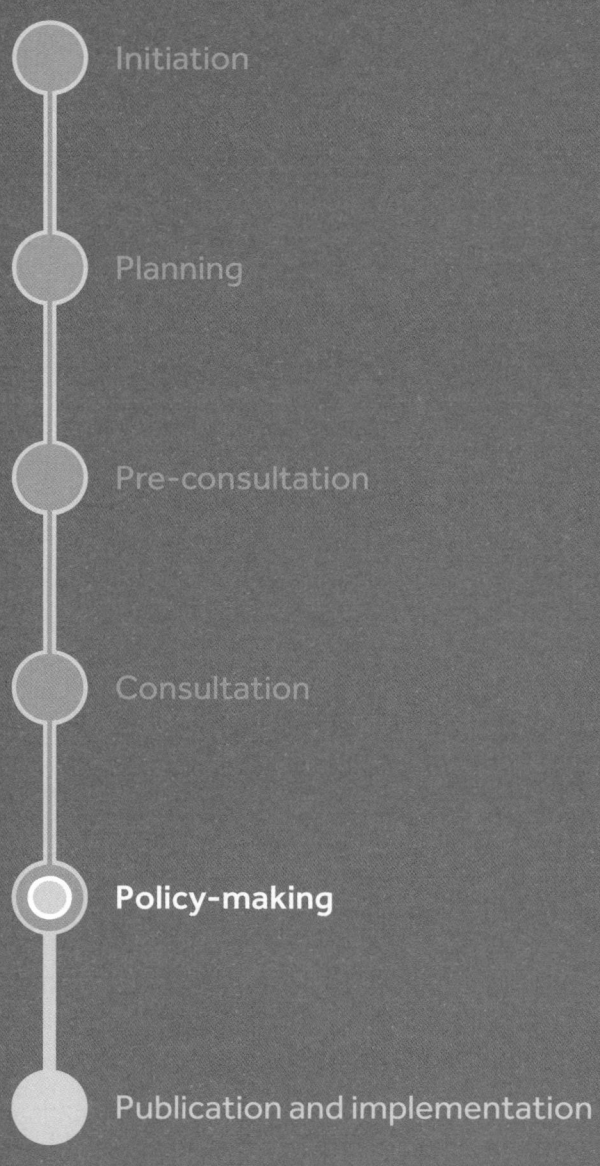

Initiation

Planning

Pre-consultation

Consultation

Policy-making

Publication and implementation

Chapter 7
Policy-making

Chapter 7 turns to policy-making after consultation. It considers how the fruits of consultation are analysed, understood and fed into the policy-making process, leading law reform agencies to come to conclusions. The chapter looks at the development of documents by which law reform project teams come to recommendations for final decisions, and how those are approved within a law reform agency. The chapter then turns to the advantages and disadvantages of cost–benefit analysis as a tool for law reformers, and considers other forms of (usually) government-inspired assessments that a law reform agency may or may not itself wish to perform. Finally, the chapter looks at how those law reform agencies that produce draft bills with their reports go about doing so.

Once the consultation process is complete, the law reform agency must come to final conclusions about what it will recommend.

7.1 Responses to consultation

The key bridge between the consultation process and decision-making is the mechanism used by the law reform agency to encapsulate and understand the responses to the consultation. Practice varies among law reform agencies. Sometimes no additional work will be necessary. In other circumstances, a fuller analysis of responses, and the results of active consultation, will be desirable.

The response to consultation is the link between the consultation process and the law reform agency's decision-making. The response may result in a written analysis.

In relation to some projects, the main fruit of the consultation period is confined to a small number of written responses. This may be the case in a narrowly focused, technical subject. In such a case, there may be no need for a further document or analysis. The responses themselves may be circulated both within the project team and more widely within the agency, as necessary, for decision.

Analysis of responses: Australia and England and Wales

The Australian Law Reform Commission prepares summaries of both written responses and consultation meetings, which are maintained on a database and organised according to the question or proposal of the relevant paper (or, for some more general responses, by chapter). When a team member accesses the database for a particular question or proposal, they receive a brief summary of each response to that question or proposal. Assuming it was received in electronic form, the summary will be linked by a hyperlink to the full response. A project team member can, for instance, print a summary document for a whole chapter to assist with the writing up of the report on that issue.

The database summaries are not separately published. While available to other commissioners, the database is seen primarily as a tool for the project team in the drafting of the final report.

The Law Commission for England and Wales produces a separate document called an 'analysis of responses' or a 'consultation analysis'. This document goes through the consultation paper chapter by chapter and proposal by proposal, both setting out quantitative information – how many consultees were for or against a proposal – and reciting the arguments deployed. These documents often include substantial quotation from responses. The purpose is to inform both the project team and, critically, the commissioners who make the final decisions (see example box 'Decision-making: commissions and institutes' at section 7.2).

For many years, the analysis of responses was a private document. More recently, the Law Commission has adopted the general United Kingdom Government approach, which requires the analysis document to be published at or before the publication of the final report. Whether publication is before or at the same time as final report publication varies.

The Commission's recent project Mental Capacity and Deprivation of Liberty dealt with the law relating to the system for the approval of steps that deprive people who lack mental capacity (in some respect) of liberty in a care context. The consultation paper received 583 written responses. The consultation analysis was published at the same time as the final report in March 2017. It deals with 95 provisional proposals and questions and runs to 297 pages. In addition, it includes a chapter on other issues brought up by respondents, which includes a section relating personal experiences of the system.[1]

The Law Commission's analysis of responses/consultation analysis primarily focuses on written responses.

It may now be good practice for a law reform agency to publish on their website a summary of consultation responses or the individual responses.

However, in most cases, it will usually be advisable for there to be some intermediate stage of assessment or analysis. This applies to both written responses and information from active consultation events.

At one end of the scale, a single, comprehensive new document analysing the responses may be prepared. This may be written from scratch or it may be the product of a computer database.

The form that an analysis or similar document takes will be substantially influenced by the decision-making process used by the law reform agency.

In some law reform agencies, a general analysis document will do no more than count the number of consultees who supported or opposed a particular option. For a more detailed understanding of the response, the team relies on each team member reading consultation responses, or at least those relevant to their own areas, in their entirety. Where this is the case, it will generally imply that the central decision-maker, such as the commission sitting as a body, will be likely to take a more high-level approach to approval.

In those law reform agencies where consultation meetings and field work by the project team will be comparatively more important, there may be a written account of these meetings or field work, but not a further distillation or analysis of the written responses.

Tanzania: The Safari Report

The Law Reform Commission of Tanzania uses the two-stage consultation approach, with an initial position paper and a more developed discussion paper. The principal focus of wide *public* consultation is the position paper. It is at this stage that the Commission undertakes field work in various parts of the country to gauge public and professional opinion. The Commission captures the information in a safari report, which informs the drafting of the background paper. The background paper is then subjected to further scrutiny at a stakeholder workshop. There is no necessity for a separate document relating to the consultation on the background paper. The safari report is not published.

7.2 Coming to conclusions: documents and approvals

In all law reform agencies, a final decision on policy must be made. The decision is characteristically made by means of the approval of a document. The nature of the decision-maker, and the practices of the law reform agency in publication terms, will determine the nature of that document.

The initial decision-making will be carried out within the project team. By whom and how decisions are made will vary with each team, and even with the personalities involved.

The law reform agency must make a final decision to recommend a policy, which will often be contained in a document. This will often form the draft of the final report.

The final decision on policy will be made by the commission sitting as a body.

However, for the most part, the locus of decision-making is the drafting of the decisive document. That is, the document on the basis of which the formal decision of the law reform agency will be based. Where a decision on some broad matter is necessary, it may be taken in advance of detailed drafting. But in most law reform projects, a series of distinct decisions must be made as each of the provisional proposals and questions are worked through, and that is usually done as a product of the process of drafting.

Decision-making: Commissions and Institutes

In all standard model law reform commissions, the final authoritative decision is taken by the commission sitting, and deciding, as a body. In standard model law reform agencies, such as the Law Commission for England and Wales and the Scottish Law Commission, the decision-making process is conceived of as including the *peer review* of the principal documents produced during the law reform process. At the Law Commission for England and Wales, while each commissioner is responsible for the work of a single-subject-matter team (see the example box 'Project teams: three law reform agencies' in Chapter 4 above), commissioners are expected to spend about a quarter of their time on the review of the work of other teams in this way. This requires a strict protocol before the meeting of the Commission at which the paper is presented. The draft paper must be circulated to the commissioners, as well as to the chief executive and senior legislative drafter, three weeks before the meeting. The commissioners must then submit written memoranda with their comments to the team within two weeks. The commissioner responsible must then circulate the project team's written response one clear day before the commissioners' meeting. The project team will be present at the commissioners' meeting, to assist with dealing with points that arise.

At the commissioners' meeting, the paper is discussed, the issues in contention having been refined by the previous exchange of memoranda, and the key issues are decided on. There is virtually never a formal vote. Sometimes issues are subject to further discussion between the project team and individual commissioners after the meeting. Provision can be made for a second commissioners' meeting, but this is not usually necessary.

At the Law Commission for England and Wales, there are two stages to the final decision-making process. The first paper after consultation to come before commissioners for approval is the policy paper. This internal document sets out the key decisions to be taken. Its approval clears the way for the team to instruct the legislative drafters to draft a bill (see below). After the bill is finalised, both the bill and the report that accompanies it are approved using the same process.

This procedure also applies to the draft consultation paper.

The Law Reform Commission of Tanzania utilises a larger meeting to scrutinise each paper that it produces. The professional meeting comprises the chair of the Commission, the full-time commissioners, the secretary (chief executive), section heads and legal officers. Once the paper has been corrected following the

In many cases, the decisive document will be the draft of the final report. Some law reform agencies however generate a distinct, internal document in advance of the drafting of the final report. Where the agency drafts a bill, this document (often a 'policy paper') will seek final decisions before drafting begins. The difference is determined by the mechanism used by the law reform agency to come to its authoritative decision. In virtually all cases, the project team will provide a recommendation.

Decision-making: Commissions and Institutes (cont.)

professional meeting, it goes to a commission meeting, consisting of the chair, full-time and part-time commissioners, and the secretary, for formal approval.

The South African Law Reform Commission appoints a project leader for each investigation, usually a member of the Commission. Research papers and final reports are developed by the Commission's research staff under the guidance of and in conjunction with the project leader and an advisory committee. All draft papers and reports are submitted to the project leader and advisory committee for initial approval before formal submission to the full Commission for final approval. The Commission retains the prerogative to comment on and refer the draft paper, or report, back to the researcher and advisory committee for amendment should this be necessary, pending final formal approval.

In the British Columbia Law Institute, each project utilises from the outset a project committee, comprising volunteer experts in the area (see example box 'Project teams: three law reform agencies' in Chapter 4 above). It is this committee that approves the draft report in the first instance. The draft report is then forwarded to the board for approval. The board, as is usually the case in the institute model, is fairly large, and comprises representatives of the key legal stakeholders whose agreement constituted the Institute, plus various *ex officio* members.

The Institute has adopted a policy that sets out the grounds on which the board may not accept the committee's recommendations. The factors include:

- the expertise and experience of the committee (the committee can be expected to be made up of those with a high level of expertise, experience and judgement in relation to the issue under consideration);
- whether a recommendation is significantly inconsistent with a previous recommendation made by the Institute;
- whether a recommendation is in opposition to an important public policy; and
- the obligation of the board to act in good faith and in the best interests of the Institute.

If the board feels that it cannot approve a recommendation, in the light of the policy, it can ask the committee to reconsider. If consensus is impossible, then the board's view is determinate. Such conflict is rare. The system requires the staff and management of the Institute to ensure that all those involved understand their roles and the expectations of them, and to monitor possibly difficult issues in order to address them before the draft report goes to the board.

7.3 Cost–benefit analysis

Cost–benefit analysis can be a useful tool for informing decision-making by law reform agencies. Such analysis aims to provide the basis for comparing different options.

Cost–benefit analysis can be a useful tool for law reformers in coming to policy decisions. It can provide persuasive arguments for implementation. However, it also has its limits.

Cost–benefit analysis is an analytical tool used to inform decision-making in relation to, for example, public policies, regulations, law reform options and capital investment projects. It can provide a very useful technique for law reformers to assess the relative advantages and disadvantages of alternative options for reform. In addition, it is increasingly the case that governments are requiring new legislative proposals (whether from within government or from a law reform agency or other source) to undergo a cost–benefit analysis. Initially, these requirements were limited to legislative proposals that affected the regulation of business, but they are becoming more general. Where this is the case, there will usually be a specific format to which these analyses must conform.

Cost–benefit analysis weighs up the anticipated costs and benefits to society, to calculate the net benefit; that is, benefits minus costs. Its purpose is two-fold: to determine whether or not a change is justified; and to provide the basis for comparing different options. Although a cost–benefit analysis is most often used when a policy initiative is under consideration, it can also be used during a project's life cycle to influence decision-making at different junctures.

Costs and benefits must be expressed in financial terms ('monetised') whenever possible because cost–benefit analysis results are expressed primarily in monetary terms. In the case of law reform, monetisation can prove challenging. For example, consider a law reform project with the objective of improving the legal procedure for establishing fitness to plead in a criminal case. It may be possible to estimate court time savings from a more efficient court procedure. However, it is not possible to monetise with any accuracy the value of increased legal certainty or increased confidence in the legal system, at least not without spending a great deal on social research.

Inevitably, costs and benefits occur over varying periods. Some will occur immediately, as is often the case with costs of purchasing goods and services to enable the policy intervention, while benefits occur in the future. In order to adjust for costs and benefits occurring at different times, a technique called 'discounting' is applied. Discounting enables the transformation of a net benefit

Cost–benefit analysis and impact: The United Kingdom and South African experience

The central government in the United Kingdom operates a unified system of impact assessment, based on, but broader than, a cost–benefit analysis approach, overseen by the Treasury and contained in 'the Green Book'.[2] This provides rules on undertaking a cost–benefit analysis, including detailed practical examples.

The United Kingdom Civil Service has a well-established governance structure to support both cost–benefit procedure and technical content. A regulatory policy committee provides civil service-wide scrutiny of cost–benefit analyses, reviewing the evidence and analyses that support policy proposals, and ensuring accuracy.

The Law Commission for England and Wales has produced cost–benefit analyses, prepared in accordance with this system, in its reports, including joint reports with the Scottish and Northern Irish Law Commissions, for almost 10 years and has a well-established internal procedure in place, overseen by a full-time economist. The Scottish Law Commission prepares impact assessments in accordance with Scottish Government guidance, but does not have an economist in post, or access to an economist's advice.

Some examples of monetised costs and benefits are outlined below:

- Training as a result of a change in the law is a consideration in all projects. In a project on the rules on unjustified threats in intellectual property disputes, one-off judicial training was costed at £131,000. In a project on the regulation of taxis and private hire vehicles, training was estimated at an initial £4.38 million with persisting annual costs of £300,000. There are rarely training costs in criminal projects because of the existing ongoing training provision for criminal case judges.[3]

- Major costs in criminal projects are usually occasioned by increases in prison places. In a project on offences against the person in 2015, the annual increase was estimated at £3.28 million.

- The most significant savings ever generated were related to a project on level crossings. The savings came about as a result of proposals that would make the closure of level crossings easier. Because this counted as capital investment, the savings were calculated on a 60-year basis. It was estimated that the net saving would be £1.4 billion over 60 years. The main source of saving was in driver waiting time, a cost given a standardised value in Treasury rules.

- In respect of some projects, it has been possible to monetise the value of increased clarity and certainty in the law. A 2015 project on wildlife law estimated a saving, based on a reduced need for external consultancy, of £2.55 million annually. In a recent project on the rules relating to the deprivation of liberty in the care of those lacking mental capacity, the Commission estimated improved health outcomes valued at £83 million per year.

In South Africa, the Cabinet, introduced the Socio Economic Impact Assessment System in 2015 in response to concerns about the failure in some areas to understand the full costs of policy initiatives, legislation and regulations. As a result, all Cabinet memoranda seeking approval for draft policies, bills or regulations must include an impact assessment, reflected in a full report that has been signed off by the national Socio Economic Impact Assessment System unit. Senior government officials representing, among others, the Presidency, the Economic Development Department, the National Treasury and state law advisers ensure quality control and capacity support for the Socio Economic Impact Assessment System throughout government.[4] All draft legislation recommended by the South African Law Reform Commission is submitted to the Socio Economic Impact Assessment System process.

into a net present value. The general rule for deciding whether or not to adopt an option is to select the project with the greatest net present value. However, specific resource constraints, such as a capital shortage, might require a more nuanced approach such as the ranking of the benefit to cost ratios for each project. Many agencies do not have the expertise or capacity to undertake proper cost–benefit analyses. Care should be taken not to undertake such analyses unless the appropriate capacity exists.

7.3.1 Advantages and disadvantages of cost–benefit analysis

A cost–benefit analysis provides transparency in decision-making by clearly identifying the basis on which decisions are made with reference to the costs and benefits to the main stakeholders. Such an approach conforms to best practice in evidence-based policy-making. It also builds institutional credibility because government officials, the legislature and citizens have access to the evidence supporting proposed policy interventions. Perhaps most importantly, a cost–benefit analysis provides for the cost-effective use of public resources.

However, it is not without its detractors. There are concerns surrounding the theoretical basis of a cost–benefit analysis. Critics question the extent to which it is possible to make a balanced assessment of gains for some against losses for others by simply netting the benefits, which amounts to trading off one person's benefits for another person's costs. One solution to such concerns about equity is the use of distributional weights, to prioritise benefits gained to those stakeholder groups identified as having particular significance. For example, participation by under-represented groups in a policy initiative may be highly valued and this might be given a weight that is twice as high as that given to other socio-economic groups that do not have the same characteristic. Such an approach provides a mechanism to adjust the outcome and address equity concerns, in an effort to ensure that the policy is fair. But, ultimately, it simply displaces the issue to the determination of the appropriate weighting.

The most frequently voiced criticisms of cost–benefit analysis surround the practicalities of applying it to the policy-making process. There are problems with monetisation when critical policy benefits lose visibility because they cannot be monetised. A cost–benefit analysis scheme may be wider than just the

Cost–benefit analysis has the advantages of transparency and providing for cost-effective resource utilisation. Its disadvantages include the problems with netting and weighting different costs, and the monetisation process. Detractors argue that many costs cannot be accurately monetised, or monetised at all.

cost–benefit calculation itself, and may provide for the statement of non-monetised costs and benefits, but by definition they cannot appear in the calculus. A proposal might be promoted because it allows for more just outcomes, perhaps in distributional terms. But this benefit is very hard to capture in monetary terms. As a result, a cost–benefit analysis may do no more than tell a policy-maker how much the enhancement of justice would cost.

Further, standard monetary values applied to things such as the value of life may also appear arbitrary.

There may also be evidential issues that tend to favour conservatism. It is often relatively easy to ascertain costs, particularly short-term costs, because these can be read off from an understanding of the status quo. Benefits, particularly longer term benefits, may be much harder to evidence, because they inevitably involve a higher degree of speculation. The danger is therefore that a cost–benefit analysis may be skewed to exaggerate short-term costs and underestimate long-term benefits.

Finally, the discount rate is very significant in determining the net present value, and small changes to it can have significant effects. But the discount rate is essentially a conventional measure, and is often based on a cross-government single standard.

7.3.2 Use by governments

Efficiency in government is said to have been the driver for techniques such as cost–benefit analysis used to seek to ensure efficient utilisation of public funds in major public investments. Most government agencies in Western industrialised economies have protocols in place that require the completion of a cost–benefit analysis as part of a broader approach to impact assessment. An impact assessment involves the comprehensive assessment of all relevant factors and includes the assessment of economic factors and also non-monetary environmental, social and political issues.

It can be argued that the potential value of a cost–benefit analysis approach in developing countries is greater than in high-income economies, because the scope for efficiency savings in decision-making may be greater. A cost–benefit analysis may also offer some insurance against corruption, in that it serves as a mechanism of transparency, making it harder for a group or an individual to distort a project plan to serve their own interests. Many developing countries now employ some version of cost–benefit analysis, but may face more challenges as a result of a lack of good data and macro-economic instability.

7.4 Other impact assessments

Human rights and equality assessments are examples of other impact assessments that some governments require.

Governments increasingly require legislative proposals or other policy initiatives to be subject to various assessments. The purpose of these assessments is to ensure that certain desirable perspectives are incorporated into the policy-making process in a holistic or generalised way. These assessments bring a variety of perspectives to bear. Very common are equality assessments, designed to ensure that policy developments do not discriminate against disadvantaged groups, and human rights assessments. But there are frequently others, reflecting the particular preoccupations and challenges of the country, such as impacts on rural areas or islands.

The approach of the Welsh Government

The devolved Welsh Government requires legislative proposals and other policy developments to undergo a number of impact assessments. Some impact assessments are required by law:

- equality and human rights;
- children and young people;
- the Welsh language; and
- biodiversity.

Others are imposed by Welsh Government policy:

- sustainable development;
- effect on rural areas;
- health;
- the voluntary sector;
- climate change; and
- economic development.

The application of the third category of impact assessment depends on the subject matter. If one of these assessments is not completed, a return must be completed explaining why not:

- privacy;
- justice and the courts;
- habitat regulation;
- the environment and environmental strategy; and
- European Union state aid rules.

Within the Welsh Government, assessments are carried out using prescribed template documents, which require consideration at each stage of the policy process.

7.4.1 Who should conduct assessments?

It may not be compulsory for law reform agencies to undertake these assessments, but there are good arguments for them doing so, where it would be advantageous.

Typically, the law reform agency will not be strictly required to undertake such assessments. In respect of an equality and human rights assessment, all law reform agencies would be expected to take account of these considerations as part of their own law reform processes. However, that is not necessarily true of other forms of impact assessment.

The question therefore is how far the law reform agency should go in performing assessments itself, or whether it should leave it to the government department responsible once they have accepted the law reform recommendations.

On the one hand, if the assessments are likely to significantly influence the department in its decision of whether or not to accept the recommendations, there is a strong case for the law reform agency to undertake the assessments itself. It is likely that the agency will do a better job of it than the department. The agency will know much more about the proposals and will have a strong motivation to see them accepted. It was this argument that led the Law Commission for England and Wales to accept the obligation to undertake the United Kingdom Government's impact assessment (which includes both a cost–benefit analysis and individual assessments).

On the other hand, if the contrary is true, then there is little to be gained, particularly if the relevant issues can be expected to be integrated into the agency's practice in any event. If the agency does not undertake assessments, it can nevertheless aim to assist the department that will undertake them with data and arguments, which may impact on consultation questions.

Even if the agency does compile the assessments itself, it will be mindful of the need to not let the process distort its own processes.

7.5 Bills

A number of law reform agencies, either as a matter of course or selectively, submit final reports with bills attached.[5] The agencies that take this approach are in the minority, but range from the larger law commissions to small state or jurisdiction agencies such as the Law Reform Commissions of Trinidad and Tobago and of the Cayman Islands.

7.5.1 Why draft bills?

There are significant advantages to a law reform agency preparing a bill to reflect its recommended changes to the law and attaching the bill to its final report.

First, those law reform agencies that provide bills find that the process of preparing a bill to implement recommendations is usually valuable. The interrogation that the proposals are subjected to as a result of the process of instructing legislative drafters assists with the refining of the policy behind the recommendations. It also helps with working out the details of the policy, for example how the proposed new law fits in with the existing common law or statutory framework. This advantage may not be quite so apparent if the bill is drafted by a law reform lawyer rather than by specialist legislative drafters. However, the process of drafting the legislation may still test the policy.

A minority of Commonwealth law reform agencies submit bills with their final reports to government. This can smooth the path of the report's recommendations into law. These bills may be drafted by professional legislative drafters or by law reform agency staff lawyers.

Presenting a bill prepared along with a report can also smooth the path towards implementation of the report. Those in government considering the report will have to hand for consideration not only the report with recommendations and the reasons for them, but also draft legislation that reflects the proposals. This provides a complete and convenient package from the law reform body for the government to pick up and consider, and begin the process of implementation where minded to do so. While, in most jurisdictions, the drafting will be revisited by legislative drafters after acceptance of the recommendations by the government, most of the hard work of drafting will have been done.

While those law reform agencies that provide draft bills are convinced of its benefits, it should be noted that there are costs to doing so. One is monetary – paying seconded drafters can be expensive. Such expenditure may only be warranted if there are good prospects of implementation while the bill as drafted remains current. Further, drafting takes time. In the case of a large and complicated bill, it can add as much as a year or more to the length of a project. This is relevant to implementation, in

Bill Drafting in New Zealand and South Africa

In New Zealand, some reports are accompanied by a bill. The Parliamentary Counsel Office has for many years provided drafting assistance to the Law Commission for its reports when it has the resources available. In most cases, however, the Law Commission's reports do not include a draft bill.

Irrespective of whether a bill has been included in a report, the administrative directives governing the government's response to a Law Commission report require, where the government accepts the Commission's recommendations, a bill to be prepared and included in the government's legislative programme. Obviously, this is a more straightforward exercise if there is already a draft bill attached to the report.

The founding statute of the South African Law Reform Commission requires that 'if after investigating any matter the Commission is of the opinion that legislation ought to be enacted with regard to that matter, the Commission shall prepare draft legislation for that purpose'.[6] To comply with this requirement, all final reports of the Commission where legislation is recommended must also contain a draft bill. The government minister responsible for the area of law to which the report pertains, as advised by their department, is at liberty to implement the recommendations contained in the report by introducing the legislation as included in the report into parliament; amend the proposed legislation before introducing it; or reject the recommendations and not introduce the legislation.

that the longer a project lasts, the more likely it is to outlast the initial enthusiasm of the government department responsible.

In the many jurisdictions where the agreed method of carrying out the law reform role is for the law reform agency to make recommendations to government without a bill, the agency may still be involved in the subsequent drafting process. The law reform body may be involved in assisting the government with the preparation of the bill.

7.5.2 The drafting of a bill

Who drafts the bill, and where they are located organisationally, differs between law reform agencies.

Some law reform agencies have their bills drafted by staff lawyers working on the law reform project in question, who provide a bill to attach to the report. This means that the agency lawyers require the skills to draft legislation, along with ongoing training and development in drafting skills. In South Africa, for instance, the research lawyers who prepare and draft the final report and recommendations also draft the legislation.

Drafting guidance can be found in the Commonwealth Legislative Drafting Manual.

Legislative counsel: Seconded, employed and embedded

The Law Commission for England and Wales seconds parliamentary counsel (as they are known) from the United Kingdom Government's Office of the Parliamentary Counsel for a period of time in order to draft bills, on the instructions of a project team, for attaching to the Commission's reports. The number of counsel seconded varies over time and in accordance with demand by the Commission and the ability of the Office of the Parliamentary Counsel to make them available.

In Scotland, the Scottish Law Commission currently engages the services of a retired Scottish parliamentary counsel on a part-time basis. He is located at the Commission and drafts Commission bills to be attached to reports. In addition, the Commission also has a working relationship with Scotland's Parliamentary Counsel Office, who draft the Scottish Government's bills. The Commission also instructs counsel in that office to draft certain Commission bills. In drafting legislation, Scotland's Parliamentary Counsel Office say that they are inspired by the Gaelic proverb 'Abair ach beagan is abair gu math e' ('Say little and say it well').

In the Cayman Islands, the staffing of the Law Reform Commission arguably reflects a fusion of the law reform and legislative drafting professions. The technical members of staff of the Commission comprise a director and senior legislative counsel. Both are legislative drafters. The same staff members therefore engage in law reform research, prepare discussion papers and conduct consultations, and then draft the bills for submission. The move from policy to drafting is seamless. Both the director and the legislative counsel also, when required, assist the government's Legislative Drafting Department in the drafting of legislation. The director and legislative counsel execute distinct roles in two substantive departments.

In many jurisdictions, the drafting of primary legislation for introduction to parliament is regarded as a specialist legal job, undertaken primarily by those who are trained in the skills for carrying out this work. There is usually a government office or unit of legislative drafters, or counsel (sometimes known as parliamentary counsel), for this purpose. The legislative drafters accumulate considerable legislative experience and skills in seeking to accurately reflect policy intentions and provide legislation that is clear to those who use it.

In such jurisdictions, some law reform agencies arrange to have legislative counsel seconded from the government office to the agency to draft law reform bills to attach to reports. An alternative arrangement is for the law reform agency to issue instructions to drafters in the government office or unit for the drafting of a law reform bill.

While each jurisdiction in the Commonwealth typically has its own legislative drafting style and possibly national legislative drafting handbooks or manuals, the common law heritage of many Commonwealth countries provides some commonalities in legislative drafting style. Detailed guidance on legislative drafting in the Commonwealth, as well as legislative procedure, preparation of drafting instructions and suggested approaches to drafting, can be found in the *Commonwealth Legislative Drafting Manual*. The handbook can be downloaded from the Commonwealth Secretariat website.[7]

7.5.3 Preparing instructions to legislative drafters

The 'instructing' of the legislative drafter is a difficult and time-consuming exercise, but one of critical importance.

Preparing instructions to legislative drafters to draft a bill to reflect law reform recommendations is a substantive task, usually carried out by lawyers on the basis of policies that have been carefully worked out and consulted upon.

For this purpose, law reform agency lawyers generally prepare a set of instructions to legislative drafters. These contain the background to and the context of the law reform project, the general policy behind the proposed reform and the detailed policy proposals to be put into draft legislative form. Although the name echoes the 'instructions to counsel' that solicitors prepare for barristers in split-profession jurisdictions, in substance instructions to legislative drafters constitute a very different sort of document. They will also be very substantial if the bill is of any great size. It is therefore highly desirable for lawyers embarking on instructions for the first time to secure training and/or to work with a more senior lawyer on a set of instructions before going solo for the first time.

When using legislative drafters, law reform agency lawyers will usually prepare a jurisdiction-specific set of instructions for them. This is a difficult and very important task, necessary to translate the findings of the law reform agency into appropriate legislative action.

Jurisdiction-specific guidance on drafting instructions is likely to be available. Such guidance will usually be written with the drafting of mainstream government legislation in mind, and may therefore need some adaptation for the law reform agency context. In general, law reform agency instructions should be easier to produce and better than those for mainstream government legislation. Unlike mainstream legislation, the

Guidance on instructing legislative counsel

Project lawyers should consult the general advice on drafting instructions for legislative drafters available in their jurisdiction. The example below is an extract from the guidance given by the Australian Government's Office of Parliamentary Counsel. It is part of a checklist of matters to which the instructor should have regard.[8]

Checklist for instructions

1.9	Instructors' details	1. Nominate at least 2 instructors. They should be people who have sufficient knowledge of the detail of the project to answer the drafters' questions and to check whether drafts meet the instructing agency's requirements and the policy. 2. It is helpful if you also state whether the instructors have any planned absences, because the drafters can then plan their work knowing when the instructors will be available. The drafters will also let the instructors know of their own planned absences.
2. The instructions: core matters		
2.1	What is to be done and why	1. This is the core of any set of drafting instructions. Start with an explanation of the key policy objectives that are to be implemented, and why legislation is needed to implement them. If the Bill or instrument is to remedy a problem with the existing state of affairs, mention this and consider including one or more examples of the problem. As mentioned above, attach any relevant legal opinions, and attach other background papers if you think this will be helpful. 2. Go on to give a complete and accurate description of how the Bill or instrument is to implement the objectives. It is not sufficient merely to paraphrase the wording of a Cabinet Minute or other policy authority. 3. Express this in clear and simple language. Try to: a. avoid specialised terms or technical jargon if possible but, if specialised terms or technical language are necessary (because of the subject matter), include an explanation of their meaning; and b. be consistent: for one concept, use the same word or phrase throughout the instructions; and c. avoid unnecessary detail or complexity (generally, it is not necessary to try to identify and address all conceivable fact situations). 4. Don't attempt to provide the exact words to be used. Instructions proposing exact words don't give the drafters the necessary information and context to help them understand why particular wording was chosen. It can also affect the amount of drafting time required to complete a project because the drafters will need to seek further instructions to understand the policy intention in order to ensure that it is being implemented effectively.
2.2	Complexity	1. Consider whether any aspects of the proposed approach may add complexity, and whether there are any acceptable alternative approaches that would be less complex. The documents on the Clearer Law page of the OPC website may help you with this. In analysing your instructions the drafters will look for areas that add complexity and will work with you to reduce complexity where possible.

Guidance on instructing legislative counsel (cont.)

Checklist for instructions

3. The instructions: other specific matters

3.1	Commencement	1. Give instructions on when the Bill or instrument should commence. Different measures in the same Bill or instrument can be given different commencements.
		Bills
		2. For Bills, the main options for commencement are:
		a. on the day of Royal Assent, the day after Royal Assent or the 28th day (or some other specified period) after Royal Assent; or
		b. on some other specified day; or
		c. on a day to be fixed by Proclamation (generally with a 6-month limit)

policy proposals for law reform are generated by lawyers with a close understanding of the legal questions involved.

7.5.4 Preparing a bill: the iterative process

Instructing a drafter is not a one-off process.

Legislative drafters work on the basis of the instructions provided to them. They consider the recommendations to be implemented in the context of the existing law, both statutory law and case law as appropriate. The drafter prepares draft provisions, in the form of a bill, and provides the bill and a note of their comments and questions to the law reform agency for scrutiny and consideration.

This process of preparing a bill is an interactive one, between those who instruct and those who draft the bill, involving a number of exchanges between those instructing the bill and legislative counsel. Counsel will frequently provide a memorandum to the project team containing draft clauses with commentary and questions, and sometimes alternative drafts. It is a considerable advantage to have drafters co-located with the law reform agency, allowing easier and more frequent face-to-face discussion. The process will usually lead to a process of refinement of the policy and the recommendations, on the one hand, and of the draft legislation, on the other.

Once both the law reform body and the drafters are satisfied that a bill would fully implement the recommendations, the bill is

Legislative drafters prepare a bill on the basis of instructions, but the process of preparing a bill involves ongoing exchanges between instructors and drafters.

then attached to the law reform agency's report and submitted to ministers or to government.

7.5.5 Explanatory notes or memoranda

Law reform agencies often prepare explanatory notes or memoranda on the provisions of a bill. These are notes explaining the purpose and effect of each provision in turn. This document is of assistance to the government in considering the recommendations and the bill. In addition, such a document is often required by the legislature to accompany and explain a bill on introduction.

Law reform agencies often prepare explanatory notes for a bill, to assist the government in processing the recommendations and passing the bill.

The form of explanatory notes or memoranda is conditioned by the use to which they are put during the passage of a live bill in the legislature. As a rule, their point is to help, first, legislators and, secondly, members of the public to understand the legislation. They should therefore be written in clear, non-technical language. Notes can also include explanatory material such as graphs and examples that may not feature in the legislation (although it should be noted that, increasingly, examples are used in primary legislation in a number of common law countries, including Australia and the United Kingdom). Notes and memoranda usually specify that they are intended as aids to interpretation and are not themselves authoritative. It is, however, not unknown for courts to consider them in interpreting statutes.

7.5.6 Drafting and implementation

Where the government decide to take forward the law reform agency's report and bill, the government may wish to adjust or not accept some of the recommendations. In this situation, the government would normally instruct its 'own' legislative drafter to amend the draft. Although it may be the same drafter undertaking the task, they would be doing so under instructions from the government rather than the law reform agency.

The resulting bill would then be introduced in the legislature by the government. The law reform agency would regard the bill as implementing their recommendations, at least in large part.

Notes

1   http://www.lawcom.gov.uk/project/mental-capacity-and-deprivation
    -of-liberty/
2   https://www.gov.uk/government/publications/the-green-book-appraisal
    -and-evaluation-in-central-governent
3   http://www.lawcom.gov.uk/project/patents-trade-marks-and-designs-
    unjustified-threats/; http://www.lawcom.gov.uk/project/taxi-and-private-
    hire-services/
4   http://www.dpme.gov.za/keyfocusareas/Socio%20Economic%20Impact%
    20Assessment%20System/Pages/default.aspx
5   Bills attached to law reform agency reports are of course draft bills, but it is
    irksome to repeat 'draft' each time.
6   South African Law Reform Commission Act 19 of 1973, section 5(5).
7   http://www.thecommonwealth.org
8   https://www.opc.gov.au/about/docs/Giving%20written%20drafting%20
    instructions.pdf. For other examples, see https://www.crownpub.bc.ca/
    Content/documents/3-DraftingInstructions_August2013.pdf; http://www.
    pco.parliament.govt.nz/working-with-the-pco#guide2.0; and http://www.
    lawdrafting.co.uk/instructions/index.php

Chapter 8

Publication, Implementation and Following Up a Report

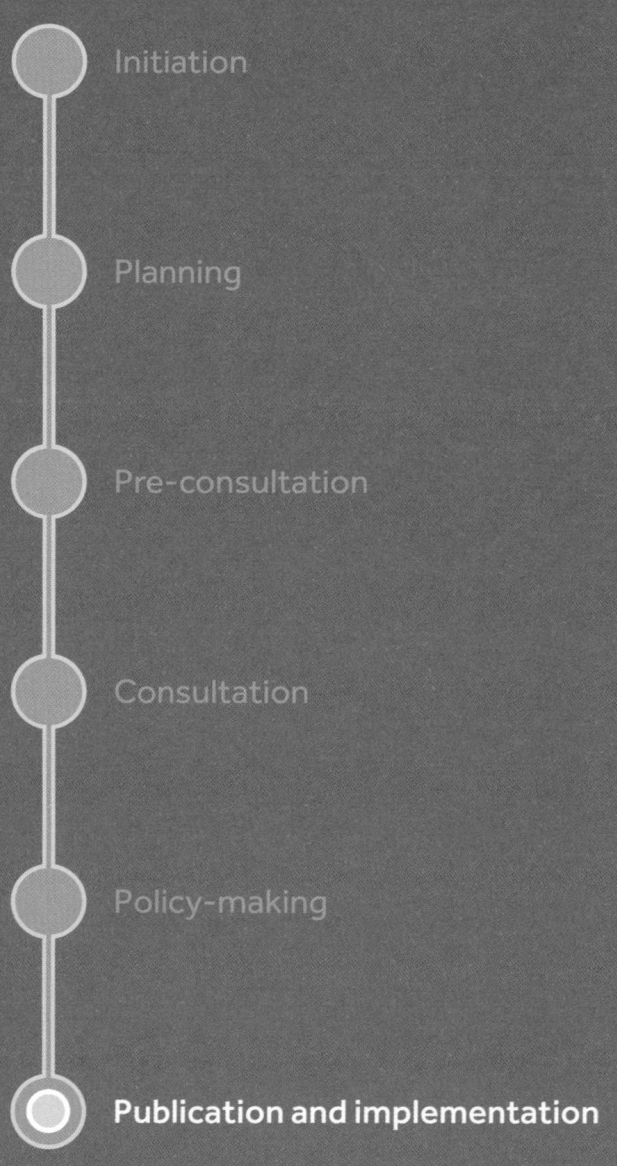

Initiation

Planning

Pre-consultation

Consultation

Policy-making

Publication and implementation

Chapter 8
Publication, Implementation and Following Up a Report

Chapter 8 covers the last stage in a law reform project – publication, implementation and following up a report. The chapter starts by considering the very real challenge of implementation to law reform agencies. It looks at the process of publication and the government's response. The chapter goes on to discuss how law reform agencies can support governments in implementing recommendations after they have been reported. This involves the consideration of possible avenues of influence, such as various forms of engagement with government and the role of supportive interest groups. Finally, the chapter considers the development in a small number of jurisdictions of a special parliamentary process for law reform agency bills, and discusses whether the model could be more widely used.

8.1 The challenge of implementation

Implementation is a key challenge for all law reform agencies. Law reform is not complete until implemented and, for the most part, implementation is in the hands of the government.

Law reform agency reports on completion are submitted to government for implementation. While the paradigm for the implementation of law reform agency reports is legislative action, it may also take other forms. These include the issuing of soft law codes of practice or guidance, changes in government policy or administration, or the development of case law by judges.

Nonetheless, most law reform recommendations are recommendations for legislation. Clearly, it follows that the objective of those law reform projects is implementation by legislation.

However, whether implementation should be regarded as the only way to measure the success of a law reform agency is a quite different question.

Law reform is not complete until it is implemented. This generally means legislative action, but not always.

Assessing the performance of a law reform agency: Implementation, but not just implementation

The primary aim of a law reform project that recommends legislative change is to see that change enacted. However, this does not mean that implementation alone is the only *measure of the performance* of a law reform agency.

The Australian Law Reform Commission has developed a sophisticated set of metrics to measure its overall performance. This includes the implementation rate, but also five other indicators. These are citation, to demonstrate the relevance of its work to litigation; the number of responses received, which shows the breadth of its evidence base; the numbers of visitors to the website and mentions in the media as indicators of community engagement; and its commitment to public debate on its work, shown by the number of presentations and speaking engagements. The Commission sets out its performance against targets in each category in its annual report. Its performance in 2015/2016 is shown below:

KPI MEASURE	2015–16 TARGET	2015–16 ACTUAL
Implementation of reports	85%	86%
Citations or references	50	56
Submissions received	150	75
Visitors to website	>250,000	1,143,519
Presentations and speaking engagements	25	29
Media mentions	250	243

The implementation rates of law reform agencies across the Commonwealth are generally commendable. One assessment demonstrates that the average implementation rate across 12 agencies, based on a study of annual reports available on the internet, was 68.3 per cent.[1]

However, a lack of, or slow, implementation of reports is a constant concern to law reform agencies. The implementation rates of some agencies are lower than others, and all go through periods of lower implementation rates. Where implementation rates are lower, this can stem from a number of factors. These include a lack of political will on the part of government, the busy schedules of parliaments, lengthy parliamentary procedures and the costs of implementing reports.

Among the reasons for slow implementation or a lack of implementation may be a lack of political will, parliamentary procedures or implementation costs.

These are objective difficulties faced by all law reform agencies. It is therefore natural that agencies and individual commissioners, board members or lawyers, who have sometimes spent years developing good-quality proposals, should be anxious to see them put into practice. But there is much that agencies can do to overcome these difficulties. That they have done, and continue to do so is attested by the value that they are accorded in most jurisdictions in which they operate.

8.2 Implementation other than by legislation

Implementation is very largely a matter of legislation, but there are exceptions.

Law reform agency reports are frequently *used* by the courts. However, occasionally, the courts may *implement* proposals.

In other projects, law reform agencies may on occasion seek to change court rules, practice directions, codes of practice or other soft law instruments, or change practice in other ways. On occasions, this may include recommending change to organisations or individuals who are not part of the state.

However, these are contexts in which, as a matter of rational legal policy, it is more sensible to seek a non-legislative route to implementation. Law reform agencies do not, and should not,

---

Implementation by the Courts: England and Wales

In its 1999 consultation paper on double jeopardy,[2] the Law Commission for England and Wales provisionally proposed that 'the rule in *Sambasivam*'[3] – that an acquittal could not subsequently be challenged in other proceedings against the same defendant by adducing evidence that they had been guilty – should be abolished, as part of the introduction of a new statutory scheme of protection against double jeopardy. The Commission provisionally concluded that insofar as the rule was a true double jeopardy protection, it was unnecessary, given the other rules, and insofar as it prevented the prosecution contradicting a previous acquittal in other circumstances, it was undesirable. In the period between the publication of the consultation paper and the report, the House of Lords considered the rule in *R v Z*,[4] and, relying expressly on the Law Commission's reasoning, abolished it in England and Wales.

The Law Commission recommended, as part of a multi-project programme of work on damages, that the courts should increase the level of general damages (for pain, suffering and loss of amenity) awarded in personal injury cases by significant percentages. Only if the courts did not act did the Commission recommend that this should be accomplished by legislation. In 2000, a specially constituted five-member Court of Appeal was convened expressly to consider the issue in a judgment on a number of appeals (*Heil v Rankin*[5]). The court accepted the Commission's broad approach, and partly implemented its recommendation for a general uplift in these damages.

Recommendations directed at other agencies

The Law Commission for England and Wales's report *Housing: Proportionate Dispute Resolution*, in addition to proposing legislative change to court and tribunal jurisdictions, proposed that advice agencies should adopt a particular approach to housing advice known as 'triage plus'.[6]

promote second-best non-legislative routes to implementation because securing legislation is difficult. So, for most agencies, most of the time, legislation is necessary for implementation.

8.3 Publication

Law reform agency reports are published and generate debate in the public domain. They are authoritative documents that can also generate specialist debate.

Law reform agencies' law reform reports are published. Publication provides the opportunity to publicise the report in the media. It provides full transparency to the agency's deliberations. When law reform agency reports are published they become available in the public domain. Consequently, they generate debate among the interested public, and provide an occasion for interested groups to make their views known.

Nearly all law reform agencies maintain a website, and will always publish their reports in electronic form. For example, most study reports finalised by the Uganda Law Reform Commission are available on the website. Similarly, over 61 reports of the Hong Kong Law Reform Commission are available online. Other law reform agencies, such as the Law Commission for England and Wales and the Australian Law Reform Commission, publish their consultation papers and reports on their websites. Most will also publish in hard copy form. In some jurisdictions, the paper publication will be available to buy through the official government publications system. Some law reform agencies, such as the Scottish Law Commission, now generally publish online only.

When published, reports become authoritative; they come to the attention of academics and are peer reviewed, a process that can generate further specialist debate. Courts and academics frequently cite law reform reports, and legal practitioners make use of the research and conclusions in the reports.

Reports should be written with their most important readerships firmly in mind. The typical readers will probably be very busy, with matters that may seem to them more important or more urgent. Those readers may very well be unfamiliar with the subject matter. It is therefore very helpful if the main importance and purpose of the report are set out near the beginning. The reader may need to be convinced from the start that the report deals with important issues and needs attention.

An executive summary may be quite as useful for many readers as the report itself. Examples, whether real or imaginary, can be helpful to readers. It may be helpful to use visual means where possible to explain and to relieve solid text, such as photographs, tables and graphs. Some detailed or optional material may be best kept in an appendix. Overly legal language should generally be avoided as far as possible.

A clearly written, readily understood report stands a greater chance of appealing to the public and to legislators who must take the matter forward.

Of all the many potential readers of a report, the single most important are decision-makers in government. It is important to recognise that it will be unusual for a minister to read all of a 200-page law reform report. Rather, this may be done by a member of the civil service or a ministerial adviser with direct policy responsibility, but by no means always a lawyer. It is not impossible that no one in government will find the time to read the whole report thoroughly before the response is agreed.

Accordingly, it is important for law reformers to ensure, first, that in the continuing process of engagement with officials during the life of the project, the officials have a sound understanding of the proposals, including the detail of the recommendations and the reasons for them. Secondly, there should be sufficient explanatory material in summary form to explain the project to those higher up the chain within government.

The publication of reports and recommendations by law reform agencies plays a critical role in ensuring that they are implemented either by legislation or otherwise. In many jurisdictions, the law reform agency relies for the publication of its reports on government authority being given or upon government printers. In some developing countries, long delays have been experienced between the submission of the report by the law reform agency and printing, and therefore publication. It is hoped that the current emphasis on rule of law issues, and the contribution that law reform agencies make to them, will

Law reform agency reports should be written clearly, with the most important readerships in mind. An executive summary will assist accessibility.

make this a thing of the past. The fact that online publication is so much quicker and easier than printing may also play a part in overcoming this problem.

8.4 The government response

Reports are addressed to the government. The government may provide a written response in return. The government may need to consult, or carry out other processes, before it can respond affirmatively.

In many jurisdictions, reports of the law reform agency are laid before the legislature. However, implementing legislative law reform proposals is overwhelmingly the task of the government, and it is to the government that the report is always addressed.

The government response to submitted reports differs from country to country. If the report is accepted by the government, the response can generally be straightforward about that acceptance. In some countries, governments will respond by providing written reasons where there is a rejection of the proposals. In others, however, the governments may not take action on proposals without any reasons being given.

Some law reform agencies have agreements or understandings with the government about the timing of the response, intended to secure reasonably timely responses. The process has recently gone a significant stage further in England and Wales (as discussed above in the example box 'Implementation by the courts: England and Wales').

As a result of amendments made in 2009, the Law Commission's founding statute now makes provision for a protocol to be agreed between the Law Commission and the Lord Chancellor. Further amendments in 2014 added similar provision for a protocol with the Welsh Government.[7]

New Zealand: Rejection requires a statement of reasons to Parliament

Since 2009, there has been a binding administrative directive in place that requires the New Zealand Government, if it rejects the Law Commission's recommendations, to respond formally stating this. The minister must present the government's response to parliament within 120 working days of the presentation of a Law Commission report to parliament. When the government accepts a Commission report it does not need to table a response, but instead begins the process of implementation, normally by having a bill drafted.

Rejection and implementation: The case of renting homes

In 2006, the Law Commission for England and Wales published a report recommending a radical overhaul of the law relating to short-term renting. It applied to the jurisdiction of England and Wales as a whole.[8] It was rejected in respect of England by the United Kingdom Government in 2008. But it was accepted by the Welsh Government, which is responsible for housing, and the Renting Homes (Wales) Act 2016 will come into force in Wales in 2017.

Both protocols make similar provision for the government to provide an interim response as soon as possible after the publication of the report, and in any event within six months; and to provide the final response as soon as possible thereafter and in any event within a year.

It is too early to know if this precedent will be picked up in other jurisdictions in the Commonwealth. It may perhaps provide at least a stimulus to governments and law reform agencies to seek to conclude non-statutory agreements along similar lines. The Scottish Law Commission and the Scottish Government have been discussing an agreement along these lines.

Governments may have a general commitment to consult before making major policy changes, including legislating. If the government seeks to consult on a law reform agency's proposals, then further delay to the government's response to the law reform agency is inevitable. If this appears to be a possibility, as part of its ongoing engagement with the government department during the project, the law reform agency may try to persuade the department that this consultation requirement has been effectively discharged by the law reform agency's consultation.

It may be that the government response, when it is made, is negative. If that is the case, then for immediate purposes the project goes into the table of projects not implemented. However, even in such cases, the project may be taken up by another government and eventually implemented.

8.5 Assisting implementation

The first stage in assisting implementation of a law reform project is for the government to accept the recommendations in the report. The second is seeing that acceptance translated into legislation.

After the government accepts a report, it needs to be translated into legislation. The law reform agency may have little formal role after the government has given its response, but can be expected to take an active interest in seeing the report implemented.

Most legislation establishing law reform agencies does not require them to do more than submit reports to government. However, law reform agencies have long expected, and been expected, to take a positive interest in the future progress of their reports. The ways in which (and the extent to which) they carry that interest forward varies considerably. In this, there are certain factors that most law reform agencies will take into consideration.

On the one hand, they will wish to retain – and be seen to retain – their objectivity, independence, professionalism and reputation for solid and comprehensive recommendations and reports. Any advice they offer will continue to be non-partisan, and will avoid jeopardising their reputation. They will seek to avoid giving an impression of entering the arena and politicising the topic.

On the other hand, they will wish to ensure – and rely upon – the high quality of their reports, including the professional manner in which they are presented, reflected by both the reports themselves and the publicity they provide. They will seek to brief the government on the report and help them to understand the problem being addressed, the views received on consultation and their recommended solution. They will also wish to encourage government to give serious consideration, within a reasonable timescale, to the report.

At some times and in some law reform agencies, there has been a view that the role of the law reform agency is exhausted once the report is delivered to government. Nonetheless, there is a spectrum of attitudes as to how far a law reform agency should go in seeking to follow up a finalised report. The great majority of law reform agencies would wish at minimum to respond to enquiries and requests for information from government.

Beyond that, it is legitimate for law reform agencies to take different views on how far they should go in respect of implementation. A great deal will depend on conditions in the jurisdiction concerned, including the formal structural relationship between the agency and government, and the agency's informal standing with the government. Some law reform agencies will take the view that any steps that could be said to go beyond clarification or briefing would risk endangering their reputation and should be avoided. Others will take the view that it is legitimate, or indeed, that it is their duty, to be more proactive in seeking to persuade government of the desirability of implementing law reform recommendations.

Practice varies markedly in this respect among Commonwealth law reform agencies. What is appropriate and advisable will not be the same in every jurisdiction, and law reform agencies will recognise and respect the fact that other agencies will, in their own national or sub-state context, make different choices.

Further, that choice may change over time. For example, a new law reform agency may be especially careful until it has acquired the reliable reputation it needs – which may take several years. Once it is more mature, and once government is more confident about its capability in producing high-quality reports in important areas of law, they may be able to work more closely together.

What is, however, critical is that each law reform agency should address the issue and develop and agree its own policy as to how far to go with regard to following up a report.

It has to be remembered that governments may not hurry to implement a law reform agency's report for many different reasons, ranging from having other priorities at that time to taking political or financial considerations into account in a way that a law reform agency might not.

The discussion in this section gives some indication of what steps a law reform agency might take. How far a particular agency wishes to go is a matter for it. This chapter is largely concerned with how agencies can successfully assist governments, over and above initial briefings.

Many law reform agencies monitor major developments on the issues that were recommended in the reports. This is done to ensure that recommendations made in the reports are fully implemented and not ignored by those to whom the recommendations are directed.

When law reform agencies submit reports to government ministries, the reports undergo a transmission process until they are enacted into law or alternative action taken. Often the transmission system may be rigid or delayed. There are therefore opportunities for the law reform agency to follow up on the reports submitted to government to assist implementation. Indeed, it has been observed that a 'law reform agency is not merely a think tank, but a body that is meant to give advice to government'.[9]

Across the Commonwealth, the transmission processes are similar. When a law reform agency finalises its report, it is forwarded to the relevant ministry. The presentation to government is intended to seek approval from the Cabinet or other responsible policy-makers.

When the Cabinet or another responsible policy-maker has approved the recommendations, where the report from the law reform agency does not attach a draft bill, drafting instructions are issued to legislative drafters to draft bills to be submitted to the legislature for consideration. Sometimes the Cabinet agenda may delay implementation of law reform reports and recommendations.

In most Commonwealth jurisdictions, bills for legislation arising from law reform proposals are introduced in national parliament or assembly for debate and enactment. Sometimes the legislative procedures in the national parliament or assembly are long. They involve committee debates and consideration of bills, consultations and plenary debates for enactment.

What follows are some indications of how a law reform agency can aid the path towards final implementation of legislative recommendations. This chapter closes with the consideration of significant new departures in two jurisdictions, which may point the way towards improved implementation rates for other law reform agencies.

8.5.1 Engagement with government

Close engagement with the relevant government department throughout the process is a key factor in successful implementation of law reform.

Perhaps the single most important element in assisting implementation is appropriate and close engagement with the relevant government department throughout the course of a law reform project.

Given that the role of a law reform agency is advisory, there must inevitably be close co-operation between the agency and the relevant departments of government. Close engagement with policy departments brings many benefits throughout the law reform process, and is of particular importance in terms of implementation. Such co-operation does not threaten the operational independence of law reform agencies, provided that the roles of both sides are understood and respected.

Establishing liaisons/partnerships with relevant government institutions is vital to ensure that law reform recommendations

Government involvement with law reform: Uganda and South Africa

In some jurisdictions, government departments are more integrated into the reform process than in others. The Uganda Law Reform Commission often appoints a taskforce or working group comprising representatives from relevant government ministries and the private sector to offer insights on the matter under consideration for reform. This helps to generate support and ownership from government departments.

The South African Law Reform Commission frequently appoints representatives of government departments as members of advisory committees where the nature of an investigation requires close co-operation with a relevant department. Such officials usually have expert or insider knowledge of the subject under investigation and are appointed at the start of an investigation, or at a later stage as the need for close co-operation and/or expert knowledge arises.

are fully considered. The Cabinet relies on the advice given by government departments. If law reform proposals are to be successful, they are likely to require championing within government, both at the departmental and Cabinet levels. And it is much more likely that the relevant policy officials will champion the proposals if they fully understand and appreciate them. It has been argued that law reform agencies' independence cannot become a recipe for isolation or non-engagement with relevant departments of the state.[10]

Law reform agencies must always work with government to develop legislative plans, where the internal mechanisms of government allow that. The publication of legislative plans would increase the involvement and accountability of all the participants in the planning for legislative processes.

The protocols between the Law Commission for England and Wales and the United Kingdom and Welsh governments make express provision for these governments to make available officials – usually a policy lead, an economist and a lawyer – with which a programme of regular communication is to be agreed. The obligations of the officials include to 'communicate promptly and openly about wider policy developments and changes in priority which may affect implementation'.

The Law Commission for England and Wales in its eighth law reform programme noted that, while it is important to preserve the independence of the Commission, the Commission has

Liaison or lines of communication should be established with relevant departments and institutions, while being sure to maintain the independence of the law reform agency.

Law reform agencies are often required to report formally to parliament or government once a year. But informal engagement can be just as important as formal reporting requirements.

developed closer links with the main government departments responsible for the legislation covered by the Commission's projects, both before and after publication of final reports. There are regular meetings with the departments, at ministerial and/or official level. Proposed projects are discussed with the department in advance, to ensure that the department is fully committed to the project and to assist the department and the Ministerial Committee on Law Reform. The Commission also keeps the department informed of progress during the project. This enables, for example, the Commission to be kept informed of relevant work planned by government and of relevant research or other studies in which government is involved.[11]

In some jurisdictions, law reform agencies are required to report to parliament annually about the progress of projects and activities undertaken. This helps the agency to bring to the attention of government and parliament any reports that are pending implementation.

Similarly, many other law reform agencies in the Commonwealth are required to report annually to either ministers or parliament on their work. This will include information about the agency's progress with its current projects. It will normally also report on the status of implementation of law reform programmes. For example, the Uganda Law Reform Commission is required by

Reports to the legislature

As a result of amendments made in 2009 and 2014, respectively, both the United Kingdom Government, in the form of the Lord Chancellor, and the Welsh Government are now statutorily obliged to report to Parliament/National Assembly for Wales on the implementation of Law Commission proposals. The statute requires the Lord Chancellor to:

'prepare a report on

    a.   the Law Commission proposals implemented (in whole or in part) during the year;

    b.   the Law Commission proposals that have not been implemented (in whole or in part) as at the end of the year, including—

        i.   plans for dealing with any of those proposals;

        ii. any decision not to implement any of those proposals (in whole or in part) taken during the year and the reasons for the decision.'

Similar provision is made for Wales.[12]

the constitution to submit to parliament annual reports of the activities undertaken.[13] Under the South African Law Reform Commission's founding statute, the Commission must within five months of the end of a financial year submit to the Minister of the Department of Justice and Constitutional Development a similar report. It must be tabled in parliament.

The New Zealand Law Commission prepares and submits an annual programme of potential projects to the minister responsible for the Law Commission.[14] An annual report is tabled in the United Kingdom, New Zealand and many other parliaments, detailing the law reform agency's activities from the previous year.

Reporting requirements are intended to ensure that a public body created by parliament is accountable. Reporting obligations aim to foster transparency and good working relationships with the government and parliament. Through reporting, law reform agencies are held accountable to government and the people. This process, in turn, may improve parliament's understanding of the law reform agency's activities and help to increase the potential for implementation of reform recommendations. The reporting function can also lead to greater public appreciation of the law reform agency's activities.[15]

Too much stress, however, should not be laid on these formal arrangements. Hundreds or thousands of reports from various sources are 'laid before Parliament' every year, and although it has a formal function, doing so has, in practice, limited impact in many countries. The strongest of these arrangements are the new requirement to report on implementation in England and Wales. In respect of those arrangements, the Law Commission has criticised the brevity and formulaic nature of the reasons given for the non-implementation of reports.

Much more important are the real but informal ties that working together on a project foster between a project team in a law reform agency and the corresponding officials in the government department. It is their commitment to the implementation of a project on which they have both worked for the public good that is key to assisting implementation at the end of the project.

8.5.2 Accompanying reports with draft bills

In most jurisdictions, bill drafting is done by a drafting office. Some law reform agencies attach draft bills to reports to encourage the adoption of the reforms.

The technical issues relating to the drawing up of draft legislation by law reform agencies have been dealt with in the preceding chapter.

In most jurisdictions, law reform agencies are not formally mandated to draft legislation for government. Bill drafting is confined to a legislative drafting office that is part of government and only drafts government-approved bills. When proposals for legislation are approved, drafting instructions are issued to the government drafters to prepare the bills. Most legislation establishing law reform agencies in Commonwealth jurisdictions does not require them to prepare draft bills to accompany reports, although in some cases, such as in Uganda, South Africa and Kenya, the legislation does require this.

Nonetheless, as is discussed in Chapter 7, a number of law reform agencies draft bills. This is intended to encourage speedy adoption of the proposed reforms by government and parliament.

When law reform agency reports are accompanied by a proposed bill, the report is able to offer the added convenience and efficiency of providing ready-made legislation to those responsible for legislative initiatives.

Further, accompanying reports with bills for proposed legislation provides an additional way of ensuring that the policy behind the recommendations is fully worked through.

Those law reform agencies that have adopted this approach regard the practice as helpful in terms of implementation. The Uganda Law Reform Commission, for example, achieved enactment of 21 of the 27 study reports submitted under its commercial law reform programme in 2010.

Where a law reform agency report is not accompanied by a proposed draft bill, it may be possible for the law reform agency to assist the in-house government drafters in the process of drafting the bill. They can assist by providing further research materials and information to the government. This can help to ensure that the government bill reflects the policy behind the recommendations and expedites implementation.

Even if a report is accompanied by a draft bill, in most jurisdictions the government department responsible will in any event instruct its own legislative drafters to reconsider the bill. It is often the case that, even if it accepts the main thrust of a law reform agency report, the government will still wish to change some details. It will also wish to obtain its own independent advice on the drafting. In addition, legislative counsel's services will be necessary during the bill's parliamentary passage to deal with amendments.

8.5.3 Media and communication

The media can play a lead role in promoting law reform and ensuring that the recommendations submitted to government are implemented. The media can shape and influence public opinion and values, generate public interest on particular issues and provide a platform for interest groups to support reforms. The media may be willing to carry stories on the reform proposals. They can provide public scrutiny and information about how the law operates in practice. It can therefore draw attention to laws that are outdated, are ineffective or contain loopholes and require reforms.

The media can shape public opinion, generate public interest on particular issues and encourage action by government and parliament.

If there is a public debate in the media, the government may experience pressure to act by implementing the law reform reports. The media explains the justification of the reforms further and exhibits the need for action.

Media exposure may also affect parliamentarians through its influence on public opinion. The media can influence public opinion in supporting the need for reforms. The media can also make it easier to keep stakeholders informed about the work of law reform agencies, increase access to publications and increase the visibility of law reform agencies to the general public. Many law reform agencies have adopted the use of media briefings, press conferences and interviews to promote and create awareness about reports submitted to governments.

Media exposure has an important role, but there are risks for law reform agencies: the media narrative could turn negative.

However, it is difficult for law reform agencies, even if they have a communications official on their staff, to handle the press when relations become difficult. There is a danger that the story will become a negative one for the law reform agency, which may damage the prospects of implementation. The lesson is that law reform agencies should modulate their engagement with the press and media according to what risks can be perceived in advance.

Nonetheless, the media can be an important tool for drawing attention to the need for law reform, serving as a conduit of information and communication between politicians and officials, parliament, interest groups and the general public.

Law reform agencies have adopted the use of other communication strategies to follow up on reports submitted to government. The development of information communication technology has widened and opened new avenues of communication that law reform agencies can adopt or use to follow up recommendations submitted to government. For example, social media today offers avenues for engagement with the public and government. Some law reform agencies have adopted the use of websites, e-newsletters, blogs, social networks, public discussion boards, Facebook, Twitter, WhatsApp and podcasts to raise the profile of reports and carry out consultations.

8.5.4 Assisting governments and politicians

Views differ on the appropriate role for a law reform agency after delivering a report to government.

It was noted above that some law reform agencies are hesitant about the extent of post-report assistance that they should undertake. This sometimes expresses itself in an assertion that law reform agencies should not 'lobby' government or parliament. 'Lobbying' is an unfortunate term. To many it conveys an implication of improper and underhand methods, which no law reform agency engages in. However, many law reform agencies regard post-report engagement with government and politicians as both legitimate and desirable. As noted above, it is for each agency to make its own decision as to what is appropriate in the light of the conditions in its own jurisdiction.

Assisting the civil service and encouraging ministers and politicians to accept innovative ideas of law reform and to obtain the necessary legislative time for reform bills may be appropriate, but are frequently unseen processes, without which the work of law reform agencies are of far less value. Progress in law reform cannot be achieved without active co-operation from those who prepare, promote and advise on legislative proposals, and so informing them of the advantages of a law reform agency's proposals may be effective.

A law reform body can establish the support of the relevant department by demonstrating the value of the proposed reform

Engaging with government: Uganda and South Africa

The Uganda Law Reform Commission often conducts seminars and workshops for Members of Parliament and government officials on reports submitted, as a way of facilitating the quick passage of the proposals.

Research staff of the South African Law Reform Commission, when requested, render assistance to the Department of Justice and Constitutional Development and other ministries in promoting legislation that results from recommendations by the Commission. Such assistance may include the drafting of Cabinet memoranda, the attendance at and participation in Cabinet meetings, the attendance at and participation in Parliamentary Portfolio Committee and Select Committee meetings, the development of amendments to bills as they progress through the parliamentary phases, the development of second reading debate speeches for ministers, and the translation of the bill into other languages.

in terms of that department's own priorities. The machinery of government must be relied upon to effectively promote those changes that a law reform agency considers desirable. To assist, law reform commissioners may brief politicians and stimulate the interests of potential champions, particularly those who have had experience in legal practice.

Positive engagement with government ministers and lawmakers can provide them with valuable knowledge about the agency's recommendations and the problems that they seek to address. This helps ministers to understand the problems and offers the necessary support to ensure government and legislative action. One form of engagement is in the form of seminars and workshops for ministers and parliamentarians. This helps to draw the informed attention of parliamentarians and government officials to law reform recommendations.

Officials in the relevant government departments play a major role in ensuring that law reform agency proposals are accepted by governments. Government officials advise ministers on the necessity of the reforms being promoted. Ministers are often willing to take on the advice given by the relevant government departments and move the proposals to the next stage.

The initiative for legislation is very largely in the hands of government. But influencing parliamentarians can still be helpful to a law reform agency. Backbench Members of Parliament may influence ministers of the same party. As such, educating Members of Parliament can be helpful in ensuring the smooth parliamentary passage of a reform bill when it is put before parliament.

In some jurisdictions, commissioners and lawyers in the law reform agency are invited to give evidence to official parliamentary committees that are engaged on inquiries into particular matters, which may relate to law reform agency projects. A particularly clear example of this is where a parliamentary committee is charged with undertaking pre-legislative scrutiny of a draft bill published by the government to implement law reform agency proposals. For law reform agencies to deploy their expertise in this way before official parliamentary committees is likely to be wholly uncontroversial.

It is sometimes seen as more controversial for law reform agencies to engage with parliamentarians from opposition parties. It is often the case that civil servants are not permitted to engage with opposition parties and, in many standard model law reform commissions, the legal staff are seconded government lawyers. Whether such a prohibition extends to staff of a law commission will depend on the particular rules obtaining in that jurisdiction. However, in many jurisdictions, appropriate engagement by law commissioners and the provision of support for them by legal staff are acceptable.

Some law reform agencies regard this form of engagement as acceptable before a report is published, but not afterwards. Others take the view that post-report engagement is both effective and acceptable.

Engaging with parliamentarians: United Kingdom

In the United Kingdom Parliament, backbenchers can set up all-party groups covering a theme, activity or cause, which can then be registered and have a semi-official role. As the title denotes, they involve politicians from all parties. The secretariat for these groups is usually provided by an outside interest or lobby group.

The Law Commission for England and Wales frequently makes presentations to meetings of all-party groups on current or completed law reform projects. For example, during the course of its project on wildlife law, commissioners and staff from the Commission made presentations to all-party groups on shooting and conservation (for which the secretariat is the British Association for Shooting and Conservation), animal welfare (secretariat: the Royal Society for the Protection of Animals), and game and wildlife conservation (secretariat: the Game and Wildlife Conservation Trust).[16]

8.5.5 Interested parties

Very often, those with whom the law reform agency consults on its law reform projects will also operate as interest groups on behalf of their constituency. Most law reform agencies would regard it as inappropriate to seek to corral such groups into an organised campaign in favour of reform proposals. But if an organisation supports the proposals, many agencies would regard it as appropriate not only to point that out to government, but also to inform the organisation itself to do so. It may be worth noting that organisations that oppose a law reform agency's proposals may very well make their views known. In respect of the Law Commission for England and Wales's project on the law relating to taxis and private hire vehicles, for instance, trade unions representing some taxi drivers held mass lobbies of parliament to oppose the proposals.

8.5.6 Private members' bills

In most Commonwealth countries, a bill may be introduced in parliament as a private members' bill. When introduced as a private members' bill, a reform proposal does not compete with the government's own legislation for a place in the legislative timetable, as private members' bills have allocated parliamentary time of their own.

However, in many, if not most, legislatures, slots for private members' bills are allocated by a ballot. It is only members who are drawn at or near the top of the ballot whose bills will have a reasonable chance of becoming law.

It may be possible for a law reform agency to use this opportunity, but in most jurisdictions, a law reform agency's report could only be appropriately passed into legislation with the support of the government. In the United Kingdom, for example, at least some of the Law Commission for England and Wales's and the Scottish Law Commission's reports that have been implemented by private members' bills have been 'hand-down bills'; that is, bills suggested to private members scoring high ballot results by the government, and, in the Scottish Parliament, members' bills. This is not always the case. The Sale and Supply of Goods Act 1994, for example, based on a Law Commission report, was a private members' bill promoted by an opposition Member of Parliament.

In some jurisdictions, it may be possible for a law reform agency to seek implementation through a private member's bill. Care must be taken to ensure that in doing so a law reform agency does not damage its relationship with government.

Whether it is seen as appropriate or acceptable for a law reform agency to seek implementation through a private members' bill, or to assist a private member who chooses to promote such a bill in its passage through parliament, will depend on the jurisdiction in question. Care must clearly be taken to ensure that, in doing so, a law reform agency does not damage its relationship with government.

It should also be noted that a law reform agency hoping for a high-scoring ballot bill will be competing with groups proposing other good causes to these members. Nonetheless, a small number of law reform proposals have proceeded in this way.

8.6 Special parliamentary procedures

A fundamental difficulty with the implementation of law reform proposals is securing parliamentary time. For recommendations that require primary legislation, normally the only route to the statute book is through a government bill to be introduced in the legislature and pass through the usual parliamentary stages.

Special parliamentary procedures ease the passage of reform proposals through busy parliaments.

Consideration, however, has been given in a number of countries over the years as to whether or not law reform body recommendations should be enacted by a special procedure, in recognition of the wide consultation process already undertaken by the law reform body, and the careful analysis given by the body to the issues and to framing the recommendations.

Some law reform bodies, and others, have called for special legislative procedures for law reform body recommendations, or at least for certain types of law reform bills, such as technical or non-controversial bills. Some of the calls have been for implementation of such recommendations by means of a ministerial order or other such instrument, albeit that the changes to be made would be to primary legislation. Alternatively, the question of having expedited legislative processes for law reform body bills has been raised frequently.

In response, governments have generally favoured implementation by the usual legislative routes. This has recognised the need to ensure proper accountability of ministers for the exercise of their powers, and to allow proper scrutiny by the legislature of law reform proposals, in keeping with the principles of the rule of law and of democracy.

Nevertheless, it may be possible to consider devising special legislative procedures for particular law reform bills that provide for the usual full parliamentary scrutiny of the bill. Special procedures may be aimed at improving the rate of consideration and implementation of law reform bills by the legislature by enhancing the capacity within the legislature in some way so as to deal with more law reform measures.

Where the legislature has a heavy workload, preoccupied with government legislative priorities and parliamentary issues, there

The United Kingdom Parliament

There is a special procedure in the United Kingdom Parliament for Law Commission bills, in both Houses of Parliament, the elected House of Commons and the appointed House of Lords.

The House of Lords procedure was introduced in order to address concerns that the rate of implementation of Commission bills had been dropping because of the pressure of government legislative business in parliament. The procedure is intended to reduce the time that a bill spends on the floor of the House, by providing for certain stages to be carried out in committee. This allows bills to be considered and scrutinised despite pressures on parliamentary time.

The House of Lords procedure was introduced on a trial basis in 2008. Two bills passed through this procedure in the 2008 to 2009 period. There was then a review and the process was formally adopted in 2010 in the form of amendments to standing orders. It has been used successfully since then on a regular basis to address and enact Commission bills.

The procedure is available for bills from both the Law Commission for England and Wales and the Scottish Law Commission.

The procedure was devised to apply to non-controversial Commission bills. What is 'non-controversial' is not defined. Any such bill is introduced in the House of Lords. There is a motion to refer the bill to a second reading committee. The second reading debate is off the floor of the House. The motion for second reading is then taken formally in the chamber. In the House of Lords, the committee stage for a normal government bill takes place in a committee of the whole House – that is, the whole of the House constitutes the committee and the sittings take place in the chamber. Under the special procedure, the committee stage is conducted by means of a special public committee. The report and third reading is in the chamber, as with other bills. The bill then passes through the usual parliamentary stages in the House of Commons, but on the understanding that it need be allocated only limited parliamentary time.

The procedure takes advantage of the fact that, at certain times in the United Kingdom Parliament's year, the House of Lords has a less heavy legislative schedule than the House of Commons.

Although they are formally United Kingdom Government bills, the government looks to the Law Commission project team to undertake much of the work of supporting the passage of the legislation, a role usually allotted to departmental civil servants. This has an impact on the Law Commission's workload.

There are also dangers with this process. The time allotted to the bills in the House of Commons is short, with the result that there is a danger that any significant opposition could prevent the bill from passing. This has not happened so far, but the danger has been real on some occasions.

may nevertheless be ways of channelling law reform business in the legislature so as to take advantage of some capacity in the system to address law reform measures. This route may be best explored by a law reform body working together with the government and the legislature.

There are examples of special legislative procedures for Law Commission bills in the United Kingdom Parliament and now also in the Scottish Parliament.

8.6.1 Scotland: a model?

A special legislative process has now been introduced in Scotland. It is worth setting out the process in a little more detail, as it may provide a model for how other law reform agencies might, in co-operation with the government and the legislature's authorities, seek to introduce a similar procedure.

Scotland has established a special legislative process to pass Scottish Law Commission bills.

The special legislative process, for a certain type of Scottish Law Commission bill, was introduced in the Scottish Parliament in 2013. A committee of the Scottish Parliament was established with a specific remit on law reform: the Delegated Powers and Law Reform Committee. This process was specially designed to increase capacity within the Scottish Parliament for addressing law reform, and thereby improve the rate of implementation of Scottish Law Commission reports.

This development opened a new era for the implementation of law reform in Scotland, with the first Commission bill going through the process and being enacted in the Commission's 50th anniversary year, in 2015.

The Scottish Parliament was established by an Act of the United Kingdom Parliament, the Scotland Act 1998, with devolved powers to legislate for Scotland on a wide range of matters.

It is a single-chamber parliament with no upper house or second chamber, a factor that has had some influence on how the model has been structured. The committees of the parliament therefore play an important role. Each committee is chaired by a convener, and most committees have between five and nine members. These are selected based on the balance of the various political parties and groupings in the parliament.

A committee can invite any person to attend a meeting as a witness. Witnesses give evidence or provide documents related to the business of the committee. The parliament has a number of mandatory committees, and sets up subject committees to look at areas of policy such as justice.

There are usually three stages of a bill:

- Stage 1: the parliamentary committee or committees take evidence on the bill and produce a report on its general principles. If the parliament agrees, the bill goes on to Stage 2. If it does not agree, the bill falls.

- Stage 2: the bill is considered in detail by a committee, or occasionally by a committee of the whole parliament. Amendments to the bill can be made at this stage.

- Stage 3: the bill is again considered at a meeting of the parliament. Further amendments can be made and the parliament then debates and decides whether or not to pass the bill in its final form.

Once the bill has been passed, there is a four-week period during which it may be challenged if it is believed to be outside the legislative competence of the Scottish Parliament. If the bill is not challenged by a United Kingdom or Scottish law officer by reference to the United Kingdom Supreme Court, it is then submitted by the Presiding Officer (a role equivalent to the Speaker) to The Queen for Royal Assent. On receiving the Royal Assent, the bill becomes an Act of the Scottish Parliament.

The Scottish Parliament decided in 2013 to make changes to its standing orders, to provide for the Delegated Powers and Law Reform Committee; and to confer a remit on the committee that includes law reform. An existing committee of the parliament, the Subordinate Legislation Committee, was renamed the Delegated Powers and Law Reform Committee; and the remit of the committee was extended to include scrutiny of certain types of Commission bills.

The Parliamentary Bureau, responsible for organising the business of the parliament, were given the power, after the introduction of a bill meeting criteria set by the Presiding Officer, to refer the Commission bill to the Delegated Powers and Law Reform Committee. This committee would then be the lead committee in scrutinising the bill.

The Delegated Powers and Law Reform Committee is given the power to refer such a bill back to the Parliamentary Bureau if it becomes clear that the bill does not in fact meet the criteria for such a bill. The parliament can then designate another committee as the new lead committee, which can take into account any evidence gathered and any views submitted to it by the Delegated Powers and Law Reform Committee.

8.6.2 The criteria for bills

The Presiding Officer of the Parliament made a determination in 2013 setting out the criteria for Commission bills for this process:

> 'As well as implementing all or part of a report of the Scottish Law Commission... The Presiding Officer has determined under Rule 9.17A.1 (b) that a Scottish Law Commission Bill is a Bill within the legislative competence of the Scottish Parliament—
>
> (a) where there is a wide degree of consensus amongst key stakeholders about the need for reform and the approach recommended;
>
> (b) which does not relate directly to criminal law reform;
>
> (c) which does not have significant financial implications;
>
> (d) which does not have significant European Convention on Human Rights (ECHR) implications; and
>
> (e) where the Scottish Government is not planning wider work in that particular subject area.'

The criteria reflect concerns raised in parliament that the remit of a new committee is not extended so as to in effect encroach on the territory of the existing Justice Committee, or to create in effect a second Justice Committee, given a previous poor experience of having two Justice Committees in place in one session. The focus of the parliament was on finding a way to address law reform bills of a certain type: ones that reform the law to reflect changes in society or develop the common law, rather than bills that are, for example, contentious or have a political profile.

8.6.3 Commission bills

Many Commission bills, emanating from useful law reform projects designed to address a variety of technical legal issues, will qualify for the process. This is subject to the proviso that, on consultation, consultees generally agree that the reform is needed and agree on the approach to reform put forward.

This process is therefore not a route for implementation of Commission bills that seek to reform the law but require decisions by the parliament on sensitive issues on which there may be a range of views within the country and across political parties.

The first Commission bill to be put into the new parliament was enacted in 2015 as the Legal Writings (Counterparts and Delivery) (Scotland) Act 2015. The second Commission bill was enacted as the Succession (Scotland) Act 2016. A further such bill, the Contracts (Third Party Rights) Bill, was passed in September 2017.

8.6.4 Assessment

There may be questions in practice as to which bills qualify for the process. It has been noted that the criteria require an element of interpretation; and also that criteria in a determination can more easily be adjusted in light of experience than can standing orders.

As the process has bedded in, and confidence in it has grown in light of experience, the criteria have been interpreted broadly.

The benefits of the process include:

- More parliamentary time/capacity is available to deal with commission reports.
- This should increase implementation of Commission reports.
- An enhanced responsibility is provided for a committee that had the expertise, and some capacity, to take on a new area of work.
- Improvements can be made to Scots law, to make it more efficient and up to date.

The establishment of the process in the Scottish Parliament has had an effect on the Scottish Law Commission:

- The profile of the Commission and of law reform has increased, within the parliament and beyond.

- The implementation of Commission bills should increase, with a dedicated process available for certain types of bills.

- There is an obligation on the Commission to identify law reform projects that will result in a bill suitable for the process. The Commission has adapted its methodology for this purpose by, for example, specifically consulting on suggestions for projects that would result in a bill for the process and being aware of the need to identify potential candidate bills from within current law reform projects.

- With regard to resources, the Commission has to provide more post-implementation support than usual to the government bill team and the committee for any Commission bill going through the process.

It took some years of steady work to increase the capacity of the Scottish Parliament to address Commission bills, by providing for the new process. This involved raising the issue of implementation and the need to increase implementation, and, for this purpose, engaging with ministers, government and the parliament by a series of meetings and events. This led to the establishment of working groups of officials from the government, the parliament and the Commission to consider the issues and find a way forward. These working groups identified a way of increasing capacity within the parliament, while respecting the sensitivities of existing committees. Finally, parliament decided to accept the recommendations for establishing this process.

The result reflects a common understanding, reached between ministers, government officials, parliamentarians and the Commission, that it is important to find opportunities for parliament to consider bills implementing Commission recommendations. The process recognises the valuable role of the Scottish Law Commission in making recommendations to improve, simplify and update the law of Scotland.

It is recognised, however, that the process is a partial answer to the issue of finding parliamentary time to implement Commission recommendations. As such, work on implementation generally, on Commission recommendations that do not qualify for the process, continues in Scotland.

Notes

1   Sir Grant Hammond, 'The Legislative Implementation of Law Reform Proposals' in *Fifty Years of the Law Commissions* (2016) ed Dyson, Lee and Stark.

2   https://www.lawcom.gov.uk/project/double-jeopardy-and-prosecution-appeals/

3   Derived from *Sambasivam v Public Prosecutor, Federation of Malaysia* [1950] AC 458.

4   [2000] 2 AC 483.

5   [2001] QB 272. See Law Commission 1999 for full report.

6   https://www.lawcom.gov.uk/project/housing-proportionate-dispute-resolution/

7   Law Commissions Act 1965, sections 3B and 3D.

8   https://www.lawcom.gov.uk/project/renting-homes/

9   Michael Tilbury, Simon N.M Young and Ludwig N G; Reforming Law Reform: Perspectives from Hong Kong and Beyond 2012.

10 'The role of institutional law reform in an open government model', presented by Maria Lavelle at Australian Law Reform Agencies Conference, September 9, 2010, Brisbane, Australia.

11 https://www.lawcom.gov.uk/document/programmes-of-law-reform/, page 51.

12 Law Commissions Act 1965, sections 3A and 3C.

13 Article 248(2) of the Constitution of the Republic of Uganda

14 Law Commission Act 1985 (New Zealand), section 7(1) requires the Commission to prepare and submit to the responsible minister, at least once a year, programmes for the review of appropriate aspects of the law of New Zealand with a view to their reform or development.

15 http://www.justice.gc.ca/eng/rp-pr/csj-sjc/ilp-pji/lr-rd/lr-rd.pdf

16 http://www.lawcom.gov.uk/wp-content/uploads/2015/11/lc362_wildlife_vol-1.pdf, page 6; and http://www.parliament.uk/mps-lords-and-offices/standards-and-financial-interests/parliamentary-commissioner-for-standards/registers-of-interests/register-of-all-party-party-parliamentary-groups/ Law reform is not complete until it is implemented. This generally means legislative action, but not always.

Chapter 9

Law Reform: Standards,
International Obligations and
Sustainable Development

Chapter 9
Law Reform: Standards, International Obligations and Sustainable Development

Chapter 9 discusses the impact of international law and standards on law reform processes, including international human rights law, as well as non-binding model laws. It also explores the important contribution that law reform can make to the realisation of the United Nations Sustainable Development Goals.

9.1 International obligations, standards, values and human rights

Law reform projects proceed on their own merits and in light of the law reform agency's assessment of the right approach. But internationally agreed values and obligations are relevant throughout the law reform process.

Countries are bound by a range of obligations under international law. They also take account of international norms and standards.

All countries take on international obligations through membership of international and regional treaties. Treaties may be bilateral or multilateral, and concluded at the international or regional level. Many multilateral treaties, or conventions, provide that they shall be subject to ratification – the process by which a state indicates its consent to be bound by a treaty, often by an act of either the executive or the legislature. Under the Vienna Convention on the Law of Treaties, where a state has signed, but not yet ratified, a treaty, it is obliged to refrain from acts that would defeat the object and purpose of that treaty.

In some countries, once a treaty has been ratified, it is treated as if incorporated directly into national law. The treaty may be relied upon directly in national courts, without the need for transformation of its provisions into specific national legislation. This approach is commonly termed 'monism'. In other, 'dualist'

Law reform can be needed to enable countries to meet obligations under international law.

countries, international law must be explicitly incorporated into national law through the enactment of legislation. Countries in the common law tradition tend to be dualist in nature.

In addition to 'hard' international law treaty obligations, non-binding, 'soft', international law may also affect national legislation. Such international law includes resolutions of United Nations bodies, such as the General Assembly and Human Rights Council, as well as concluding observations of treaty bodies, such as the United Nations Human Rights Committee and the Committee on the Rights of the Child, responsible for monitoring the implementation of the International Covenant on Civil and Political Rights and the United Nations Convention on the Rights of the Child, respectively.

As well as hard and soft international law, international and regional organisations also produce a wide range of non-binding standards and guidance, including, in particular, model laws. As described below, the Commonwealth Secretariat, for example, has produced around 20 model laws across a number of legal areas.

Many international treaties require (at least in dualist systems) legislative provisions. The United Nations Convention against Corruption, for example, requires states parties to 'adopt such legislative measures' as may be required to establish a number of acts as criminal offences, including bribery of public officials, embezzlement by public officials, the misappropriation or other diversion of property by a public official, trading in influence, abuse of functions, illicit enrichment, bribery and embezzlement in the private sector, laundering and concealment of proceeds of crime, and the obstruction of justice.

Legislative amendments required by an international treaty are usually a matter for the executive and legislature as a central component of the process of treaty ratification. On occasion, however, law reformers review areas of law where binding treaty law, soft international law or non-binding standards produced by either international or regional organisations are relevant. It is important for law reformers to have a broad appreciation of international law and to research and examine the extent to which, if at all, international law and standards affect the current law and any possible reforms to that law. The Australian Law Reform Commission Act 1996, for example, provides 'In performing its functions, the Commission must aim at ensuring that the laws, proposals and recommendations it reviews, considers or makes...

are, as far as practicable, consistent with Australia's international obligations that are relevant to the matter' (section 24).

Research on relevant international law and standards can be carried out an early stage in research on a law reform project. Where a country is already party to a treaty, the requirements of the treaty should in principle (in dualist systems) already be reflected in existing national law. Treaties often have a range of optional provisions or open modes of implementation, however, and there may well remain significant scope for further implementation or inclusion of optional provisions in legislation. In addition to binding treaty provisions, a large number of areas of law are addressed by soft international law and non-binding recommendations and standards. These may provide a higher level of detail regarding options for legislative approaches than shorter, negotiated treaty provisions. Some standards may have specific relevance to a multilateral treaty. Others may deal with a topic in respect of which no international convention exists, such as in the case of the Basic Principles on the Use of Force and Firearms by Law Enforcement Officials[1] or the United Nations Principles for Older Persons.[2]

Law reform and international obligations

International treaties, standards and instruments that are relevant to a project can be reviewed and explained in the consultation document as well as in the final report. Examples are outlined below.

The South African Law Reform Commission provided a detailed discussion of the significance, to laws affecting prostitution, of international human rights, including several international instruments, in its discussion paper *Sexual Offences – Adult Prostitution*.[3]

That Commission, in its August 2002 report *Review of Security Legislation (Terrorism: Section 54 of the Internal Security Act, 1982 (Act No 74 of 1982))*, also analysed and sought to bring South African legislation for combating terrorism in line with the international conventions and instruments dealing with terrorism.[4]

In its work on the criminal law centred around children's non-accidental death or serious injury, the Law Commission for England and Wales considered in detail the vital importance of international obligations both to ensure fair trials and to protect the fundamental human rights of children.[5]

In its work on official secrets, the Law Commission for England and Wales examined the impact of the right of freedom of expression.[6]

The Uganda Law Reform Commission has been entrusted with a different role: it has been designated by the Attorney-General as the country co-ordinator on matters relating to the United Nations Commission on International Trade Law, the core United Nations legal body for international commercial law.[7]

Three specific areas of international law and policy that may be particularly relevant to law reformers are Commonwealth standards, international human rights law, and the 2030 Agenda for Sustainable Development. These are detailed further below.

9.1.1 Commonwealth standards

The Commonwealth Charter, adopted in 2013, sets out the values of the Commonwealth. These values include a commitment to upholding and strengthening the rule of law.

The Commonwealth's values and principles are set out in the Commonwealth Charter, adopted in 2013.[8] These values and principles are also embedded in preceding Commonwealth declarations, notably the Singapore Declaration on Commonwealth Principles (1971)[9] and the Harare Commonwealth Declaration (1991).[10] They confirm the Commonwealth's commitment to promoting democracy and good governance, human rights and the rule of law, gender equality, and sustainable economic and social development. Of particular relevance is this statement on the rule of law:

> *We believe in the rule of law as an essential protection for the people of the Commonwealth and as an assurance of limited and accountable government. In particular we … recognise that an independent, effective and competent legal system is integral to upholding the rule of law, engendering public confidence and dispensing justice.*

In seeking to uphold the Commonwealth Charter in their work, law reformers will take into account, in line with the United Nations definition of the rule of law,[11] many principles. They include equality before the law, accountability to the law, fairness in the application of the law, separation of powers, participation in decision-making, legal certainty, avoidance of arbitrariness, and procedural and legal transparency. Such principles will find expression and application across a wide range of laws, including areas of criminal and public law.

The Commonwealth has worked, in particular, on principles for the *separation of powers* as a key component of the rule of law. The Commonwealth (Latimer House) Principles on the Three Branches of Government[12] highlight, for example, the importance of providing the opportunity for public input into the legislative process.

The Latimer House Principles set out the importance to the rule of law of maintaining the separation of powers.

In addition to these high-level principles, the Commonwealth has developed concrete legal policy guidance for countries in the form of Commonwealth model laws and provisions in selected legal areas. Commonwealth model laws and provisions represent a non-binding technical resource that countries can draw upon in the development of new legislation. Model laws and provisions are developed by utilising experience from across the Commonwealth and are approved through an inter-governmental process by meetings of all Commonwealth law ministers. This provides Commonwealth model laws and provisions with a level of authority that represents the combined legal knowledge and experience from across the Commonwealth. Model laws and provisions are often accompanied by commentary and implementation guidelines. Where law reformers work on a topic in which a Commonwealth model law exists, the model can provide concrete guidance as to legislative practice and legal policy approaches.

The box below lists all Commonwealth model laws and provisions, as of the date of this publication. These models may be accessed via the Commonwealth Secretariat website.[13]

The Commonwealth Secretariat and others have produced model laws across a range of legal areas, to assist Commonwealth countries with law reform.

Commonwealth model laws

- Common Law Legal Systems Model Legislative Provisions on Money Laundering, Terrorism Finance, Preventive Measures and Proceeds of Crime 2017
- Model Law on Judicial Service Commissions 2017
- Model Law on Foreign Judgments 2017
- Model Legislation on Mutual Legal Assistance 2014
- Model Act on Integrity in Public Life 2013
- Model Act on Criminal Disclosure and Model Prosecution Disclosure Guidelines 2011
- Model Law on the Implementation of the Rome Statute 2011
- Model Legislative Provisions on Whistleblowing 2008
- Model Law on Competition 2005
- Model Law on the Protection of Personal Information 2005
- Model Bill on Freedom of Information 2002
- Model Law on Privacy 2002
- Model Law on Computer and Computer-related Crime 2002
- Model law on Electronic Transactions 2002
- Model law on Electronic Evidence 2002
- Model Law on Evidentiary Provisions 2002
- Model Legislative Provisions on Terrorism 2002
- Model Bill for the Protection of Cultural Heritage 1999

In addition to model laws developed by the Commonwealth, a number of other international organisations have also created model laws and provisions on a wide range of legal topics. These include the Model Law on International Commercial Arbitration 1985 (amended in 2006), developed by the United Nations Commission on International Trade Law; Model Clauses for the Use of the Principles of International Commercial Contracts 2017 and the Model Law on Leasing 2008, developed by the International Institution for the Unification of Private International Law; the Model Law on the Protection of Cultural Property in the Event of Armed Conflict and the Model Law on the Geneva Conventions, developed by the International Committee of the Red Cross; and Model Legislative Provisions against Organized Crime, the Model Law against Trafficking in Persons, the Model Law on Extradition 2004, the Model Law on Mutual Assistance in Criminal Matters 2007, Model Legislative Provisions on Drug Control, and the Model Law on Witness Protection, developed by the United Nations Office on Drugs and Crime.

9.1.2 Human rights

The Commonwealth Charter commits member countries to uphold international human rights standards.

In addition to the principle of the rule of law, the Commonwealth Charter also commits member countries to upholding international human rights standards:

> *We are committed to the Universal Declaration of Human Rights and other relevant human rights covenants and international instruments. We are committed to equality and respect for the protection and promotion of civil, political, economic, social and cultural rights, including the right to development, for all without discrimination on any grounds as the foundations of peaceful, just and stable societies. We note that these rights are universal, indivisible, interdependent and interrelated and cannot be implemented selectively.*

International human rights law consists of an extensive body of treaty law, as well as soft international law, in the form of resolutions of the Human Rights Council and jurisprudence of human rights treaty bodies and special rapporteurs. In addition to human rights treaties concluded under the auspices of the United Nations, three regional systems of human rights law exist: the African Charter on Human and Peoples' Rights, the European Convention on Human Rights and the Inter-American Convention on Human Rights.

As a matter of international law, countries are bound by the obligations contained within the specific human rights treaties to which they are party. In addition, countries should have regard to international human rights standards and recommendations developed through the work of the Human Rights Council, including outputs of the Universal Periodic Review mechanism.[14] As with other areas of international law, human rights treaty law and standards can require countries to put in place specific legislative provisions, including, in some cases, criminal provisions, as well as mechanisms for accountability and remedies in the case of human rights violations. In addition, human rights treaty bodies emphasise the importance of ensuring that all national legislation is consistent with and promotes the realisation of those rights that the state is obligated to respect, protect and fulfil by virtue of membership of a human rights treaty.

Ensuring the consistency of legislation with international human rights law is a complex undertaking. The state, represented by its government, has overall responsibility at the international level for its human rights obligations. At the national level, the executive, the legislature and the judiciary all have a role to play in contributing to this task. In addition, in many countries, national human rights institutions support the state in promoting and protecting human rights. The Paris Principles on the Status of National Institutions,[15] adopted by both the United Nations Human Rights Council and the General Assembly, provide that national human rights institutions 'shall examine the legislation and administrative provisions in force, as well as bills and proposals, and shall make such recommendations as it deems appropriate in order to ensure that these provisions conform to the fundamental principles of human rights; it shall, if necessary, recommend the adoption of new legislation, the amendment of legislation in force and the adoption or amendment of administrative measures'.

While national human rights institutions may have such a function under national law, this does not mean that a law reform agency need not take international human rights law into account in its own work. International human rights standards touch on almost all aspects of national law, in particular through the wide reach of rights to private and family life, as well as freedoms of association and expression. In this regard, it is important for law reformers to understand the human rights treaty obligations undertaken by their country. Key human rights treaties whose ratification status should be checked include:

Law reform can be needed to ensure compliance with international human rights law. Law reform agencies can work with national human rights institutions to deliver these reforms.

- the International Covenant on Civil and Political Rights, 1966;

- the International Covenant on Economic, Social and Cultural Rights, 1966;

- the International Convention on the Elimination of all forms of Racial Discrimination, 1965;

- the Convention on the Elimination of all forms of Discrimination Against Women, 1979;

- the United Nations Convention Against Torture and other Cruel, Inhuman and Degrading Treatment or Punishment, 1984;

- the United Nations Convention on the Rights of the Child, 1989;

- the International Convention on the Protection of the rights of all Migrant Workers and Members of their Families, 1990;

- the International Convention for the Protection of All Persons from Enforced Disappearances, 2006; and

- the Convention on the Rights of Persons with Disabilities, 2006.

In order to understand the way in which treaty-based rights have been interpreted and applied in the national context, a key resource to be consulted by law reformers is the universal human rights index.[16] This provides searchable access to information from the United Nations human rights system, including treaty bodies, special procedures of the Human Rights Council, and the Universal Periodic Review. Law reformers may, for example, search the index for key terms associated with the legal topic on which they are working, in order to identify relevant human rights standards and issues.

9.1.3 The 2030 Development Agenda and the Sustainable Development Goals

In September 2015, member states of the United Nations adopted the 2030 Agenda for Sustainable Development, together with the Sustainable Development Goals. While not having the same status as treaty law, all countries are committed to the realisation of the Sustainable Development Goals at national level, as well as through reporting and monitoring processes at international level.[17] The Sustainable Development Goals represent global sustainable development aspirations until 2030 across all of the economic, social and environmental aspects of development.

There are 17 Sustainable Development Goals consisting of 169 targets. As discussed in the next section of this chapter, national law can contribute to the realisation of multiple of these targets. Sustainable Development Goal 16, on just, peaceful and inclusive societies, however, has particular relevance to law reformers in two important respects. On the one hand, Goal 16 contains key targets, mostly in the criminal sphere, related to the reduction of violence, corruption and illicit financial flows. As with goals and targets in other areas, the work of law reformers can develop or strengthen national laws that play a key role in the realisation of such targets. This could include, for example, the reform of laws on bribery, or on public accounting, procurement, or financial system regulation and transparency.

In addition to work on specific reform projects, the very *existence and functioning* of a law reform entity *itself* contributes to the realisation of Goal 16 targets related to effective, accountable and transparent institutions, as well as responsive, inclusive, participatory and representative decision-making. In conducting its work with due regard to principles such as broad consultation and effectiveness in legal policy-making, the law reform entity can play a key role in the realisation of the country's overall responsibilities under Goal 16.

Most broadly, every law reform entity has the opportunity to contribute to the realisation of the whole range of sustainable development goals and targets. Law reform entities may take a proactive approach in this regard. In addition, for example, to considering intersections with individual Sustainable Development Goal targets for existing law reform projects, law reform agencies may consider using the Sustainable Development Goals to guide priorities for future work programmes. This may include undertaking reviews and research on areas of law where reform may benefit the realisation of the Sustainable Development Goals. It could also include initiating a dialogue between law reform bodies, national parliaments, civil society and key stakeholders,

Law reform is one mechanism to assist achieving the Sustainable Development Goals (SDGs), particularly SDG 16 on just, peaceful and inclusive societies.

regarding linkages between legal frameworks, national development plans and those Sustainable Development Goals that represent a particular national priority.

In this way, law reformers can play a key role in promoting sustainable development processes. The next section examines, in more detail, the relationship between law and sustainable development, with a view to providing law reformers with perspectives on how their work can promote development, across a range of thematic legal areas.

9.2 Law reform and sustainable development

Under Sustainable Development Goal 16, the rule of law and access to justice is recognised as a development *end* in itself within the 2030 Agenda. In addition, however, the rule of law also plays a key role in *enabling* other sustainable development goals and targets.

The rule of law is an enabler of sustainable development, through: legal frameworks, institutional capacity and legal empowerment. These components intersect with the economic, social and environmental dimensions of sustainable development.

Drawing from the United Nations definition of the rule of law, the concept of the rule of law can be thought of as consisting of three components: legal frameworks, institutional capacity and legal empowerment. Each of these three components intersects with the *economic*, *social* and *environmental* dimensions of sustainable development.

National legal frameworks, for example, commonly touch upon all three dimensions of sustainable development. Laws on commerce, finance, competition, trade, investment and legal entities regulate *economic* transactions and contracts, ownership, property, and access to financial resources and markets, engaging Sustainable Development Goal 8.[18] Criminal law, public and administrative law, and laws on education and health regulate *social* behaviour, legal identity and access to justice, as well as access to medical services and social rights, affecting fulfilment of not only Sustainable Development Goal 16, but also Goals 3 and 4.[19] Regulatory, criminal and procedural law impact upon *environmental* protection, use and access to natural resources such as water, minerals and forests, and climate change adaptation and mitigation, impacting on the realisation of Goals 13, 14 and 15.[20]

Both national and international law have the potential for positive – and, in some cases, negative – impacts upon sustainable development. In the economic sphere, for instance, sound legal frameworks can increase clarity, certainty and the predictability of business transactions, or secure land title or balance investment incentives. This, in turn, promotes increased confidence in investment and business, and generates an enabling environment for economic growth.

Across the Commonwealth, expert advisers, supported by the Commonwealth Fund for Technical Co-operation, report the importance of sound legal frameworks for sustainable economic growth. In one Caribbean country, for example, support for the drafting of a Public Procurement Act and a Public Finance Management Act; the development of a framework for contract management and administration; as well as legal advice on the commercialisation of government estates through a public–private partnership have been associated with a recent generation of employment, a reduction in unemployment and growth in the construction sector.

In the social sphere, effective legal frameworks can ensure the legal identity of individuals, allowing access to education, health and employment. Laws can set out commonly accepted standards of behaviour in the form of criminal legislation, combat discrimination in access to goods and services, ensure access to information and provide access to justice, including both formal and informal means of dispute resolution. Such outcomes facilitate the full inclusion and equal rights of all groups and individuals in society, empowering persons to be economically and socially active. As regards legal identity, in particular, Sustainable Development Goal target 16.9 commits states to 'provide legal identity for all, including birth registration'.

In the environmental sphere, legal frameworks with effective enforcement mechanisms can prevent and provide redress in the case of environmental pollution, provide rights to participation for local communities and indigenous persons in the use of natural resources, and set targets and standards for limiting environmental deterioration. Such outcomes can be critical to protecting, restoring and promoting the sustainable use of ecosystems, sustainably managing forests, combating desertification, halting and reversing land degradation and biodiversity loss, and promoting climate change adaptation and mitigation.

There are particular areas of law which are important in assisting sustainable development.

When laws are unclear, inconsistent or ambiguous, however, they can hinder commercial transactions, sustainable land use, social welfare or crime prevention, or they might enforce traditional social codes that discriminate against poor and vulnerable groups. At best, this may mean a missed opportunity for sustainable development. At worst, it could actively hinder development. In some cases, countries may not possess laws that adequately protect interests such as water management and sanitation, energy generation and distribution, agricultural development, and protection against environmental pollution and degradation. Legal systems that do not adequately cover intellectual property and technology transfer issues may further result in only marginal benefit from advances in science, technology and innovation that could assist in addressing development challenges.[21]

The conceptual connections between the rule of law and development are clear. However, when it comes to individual *country-level* law reform and the strengthening of legal frameworks, it may sometimes be challenging to identify those reforms that might be of most benefit for sustainable development. There remains the question, in effect, of which areas of law should be prioritised in order to achieve the greatest overall sustainable development gains.

This question is, of course, far from straightforward and – in each country context – must take into account a number of different factors. These include particular national Sustainable Development Goal and target priorities, national strengths and challenges in the justice system, and the overall evidence base for the relationship between particular legal provisions and specific development outcomes. Such research may be beyond the scope of most law reform agencies, although law reform agencies may play an important role in advocating and collaborating in such research.

While further research is needed, a few, indicative, areas of law that law reform agencies may consider as particularly important to sustainable development include legal identity, company and commercial law, and climate change law. Laws on birth registration, data protection, identity theft and digital identity, for example, can all support the realisation of Sustainable Development Goal target 16.9: 'provide legal identity for all, including birth registration'. In the area of climate change, overarching climate change statutes, energy market laws, greenhouse gas emissions laws, and land use and forestry laws can all support Sustainable Development Goal 13: 'take urgent action to combat climate change and its impacts'. Closely related to this, disaster risk management laws may support Sustainable Development Goal target 13.1: 'strengthen resilience and adaptive capacity to climate-related hazards and natural disasters in all countries'. In the area of commercial and company law, laws related to the registration and operation of companies, debt and equity finance, secured transactions and corporate insolvency can support Sustainable Development Goal target 8.1: 'sustain per capita economic growth in accordance with national circumstances and, in particular, at least seven per cent gross domestic product growth per annum in the least developed countries'. In addition, legal frameworks on innovation and intellectual property, traditional knowledge and genetic resources have a direct bearing on Sustainable Development Goal target 15.6 – 'promote fair and equitable sharing of the benefits arising from the utilisation of genetic resources and promote appropriate access to such resources, as internationally agreed' – and target 9.b – 'support domestic technology development, research and innovation in developing countries, including by ensuring a conducive policy environment for, inter alia, industrial diversification and value addition to commodities'.

There is no 'one-size-fits-all' approach when it comes to legal reform and development, and the examples above represent only a very small proportion of laws that may have relevance to sustainable development. Further research in this area is needed. In seeking to maximise the role of law reform in promoting sustainable development, however, law reform entities may consider actions such as examining options for undertaking a high-level 'mapping' of legal frameworks and possible intersections with Sustainable Development Goal targets, as well as possibilities for developing a national 'roadmap' for law reform in support of sustainable development.

Notes

1 http://www.ohchr.org/EN/ProfessionalInterest/Pages/UseOfForceAnd Firearms.aspx

2 http://www.ohchr.org/EN/ProfessionalInterest/Pages/OlderPersons.aspx

3 http://salawreform.justice.gov.za/reports/r-pr107-SXO-AdultProstitution-2017-Sum.pdf

4 http://www.justice.gov.za/salrc/reports/r_prj105_2002aug.pdf

5 https://www.lawcom.gov.uk/project/children-their-non-accidental-death-or-serious-injury-criminal-trials/; see Part IV.

6 https://www.lawcom.gov.uk/project/protection-of-official-data/, chapter 6.

7 http://www.uncitral.org/

8 http://thecommonwealth.org/our-charter

9 http://thecommonwealth.org/history-of-the-commonwealth/singapore-declaration-commonwealth-principles

10 http://thecommonwealth.org/history-of-the-commonwealth/harare-commonwealth-declaration

11 http://www.un.org/Docs/journal/asp/ws.asp?m=S/2004/616

12 http://thecommonwealth.org/sites/default/files/history-items/documents/LatimerHousePrinciples.pdf

13 www.thecommwealth.org

14 http://www.ohchr.org/EN/HRBodies/UPR/Pages/UPRMain.aspx

15 http://www.ohchr.org/EN/ProfessionalInterest/Pages/StatusOfNational Institutions.aspx

16 http://uhri.ohchr.org

17 https://sustainabledevelopment.un.org/hlpf

18 Sustainable Development Goal 8: Promote sustained, inclusive and sustainable economic growth, full and productive employment and decent work for all.

19 Sustainable Development Goal 3: Ensure healthy lives and promote well-being for all at all ages; Sustainable Development Goal 4: Ensure inclusive and equitable quality education and promote lifelong learning opportunities.

20 Sustainable Development Goal 13: Take urgent action to combat climate change and its impacts; Sustainable Development Goal 14: Conserve and sustainably use the oceans, seas and marine resources for sustainable development; Sustainable Development Goal 15: Protect, restore and promote sustainable use of terrestrial ecosystems, sustainable manage forests, combat desertification, and halt and reverse land degradation and halt biodiversity loss.

21 See, for example, International Development Law Organization, 2014.

Chapter 10

Law Reform in Small States

Chapter 10
Law Reform in Small States

Chapter 10 turns to the particular challenges of law reform in small Commonwealth states and jurisdictions. Of the 52 members of the Commonwealth, 30 are classified as small states. In addition, law reform agencies exist in a number of non-state jurisdictions. Chapter 10 covers the challenges and advantages of a small population and land area, and the impact that can have on the structure of law reform agencies there, including the particular pressures on staffing. The chapter looks at how such agencies adapt the law reform process, and the particular significance of comparative research for them. It goes on to outline how, despite the challenges, small state and jurisdiction law reform agencies have made very considerable contributions to the law. Finally, the chapter assesses the particular utility of co-operation between law reform agencies, including through regional associations.

The globalisation and internationalisation of law has far-reaching implications for researchers, practitioners, policy-makers and reformers. Whether in a small state or large one, a law reform agency is able to take an inclusive, objective and professional approach to the reform of the laws that govern society. It is particularly suited to topics where independent, non-partisan investigation would assist in establishing the credibility of law reform proposals, or where collaboration or consultation with a wide range of stakeholders is needed. Projects undertaken by a law reform agency are usually substantial, possibly involving new concepts or fundamental review, which government agencies are sometimes unable to undertake because of time constraints and the electoral cycle. As an institution, a law reform agency, whatever the size of the jurisdiction, must always identify new concepts and new approaches to law, and consider ways of enhancing

There are specific challenges and advantages involved in conducting law reform in small states.

Small states have to make difficult choices about allocating scarce resources. There is value in investing in a law reform agency because the benefits can extend beyond the justice sector.

the engagement of the community it serves with the law and public institutions. This requires, of the law reform agency, that it periodically re-designs its methodology so that it remains creative and responsive.

Of the 52 members of the Commonwealth, 30 are classified as small states. As with other issues, law reform in small states (and non-state jurisdictions) has particular challenges, but also advantages.

Small states, for these purposes, are defined as those with a population of fewer than 1.5 million people. Some larger countries – Botswana, Jamaica, Lesotho, Namibia and Papua New Guinea – are also classified as small states, as they have similar characteristics.

A number of small states and other jurisdictions within the Commonwealth have established law reform agencies by statute: the Bahamas, the British Virgin Islands, the Cayman Islands, Dominica, Fiji, Jersey, Lesotho, Mauritius, Namibia, Papua New Guinea, Samoa, the Solomon Islands, Tonga, Trinidad and Tobago, and Vanuatu. Most of these are still in place. They are all standard model law reform agencies.[1]

Establishing a law reform agency in a small state or jurisdiction may appear as a low priority activity when weighed against competing pressures to establish and support other justice agencies, initiatives and programmes that build capacity in the public sector. However, there are multiple long-term benefits in investing scarce resources in a law reform agency that extend beyond the justice sector. A well-designed programme can build much-needed legal policy skills that can become a resource for the use of other public sector ministries and government.

10.1 The challenges of law reform in small states and jurisdictions

Limited financial and human resources pose significant challenges to law reform in small states.

Despite their heterogeneity, small states share the constraint of 'smallness' – that is, a small population, limited human capital, the lack of economies of scale, a constrained domestic market, and increasing exposure to climate change and market shocks. Most small states have small land areas.

Many of the challenges faced by law reform agencies are very similar whether the institution serves a large or a small country. However, there are additional issues for small states and jurisdictions. Limited financial and human resources with a lack of the required local expertise in all sectors to enable specialised and effective law reform are some of the major challenges for law reform in small states. In order to undertake the many obligations imposed on a law reform agency, high-quality personnel are required. It may be difficult for an agency to attract and retain suitable persons, and to commit resources for the continuous capacity building of the institution.

Law reform agencies in small states also face the challenge of developing appropriate and effective law reform processes to ensure maximum input from stakeholders, thereby ensuring the agency's responsiveness to the developing needs of society.

Fostering the trust of stakeholders, and maintaining independence and neutrality, can be particularly challenging in small states.

A further major challenge for a law reform agency in a small state is to foster trust and confidence among all its stakeholders in its usefulness and the necessity of its existence as an independent and politically neutral agency. There is a need to cultivate political goodwill in support of its activities, the more so given the particularism of relationships in small jurisdictions. A Commonwealth Secretariat paper on small states and law reform notes:

> *A major challenge for smaller [law reform agencies] is to cultivate political will. On occasion a government may suspect that [a law reform agency] is inclined to advance either a donor agenda or the opposition agenda, due to the [law reform agency's] independence from mainstream government and its unusual funding arrangements. On the other hand, others may on occasion suspect that a government uses its [law reform agency] mainly as an indication of its democratic credibility and as a means of securing donor aid rather than recognising the [law reform agency] for what it is.[2]*

There may also be the challenge of living up to expectations. This requires keeping up with demand by avoiding taking on too many projects for their limited capacity. An allied criticism often levelled against law reform agencies is that time frames are unduly long. The agency can be faced with the challenge of convincing government, stakeholders and donors that adequate time frames are necessary to allow for proper research and consultations and that these processes are indispensable in law reform.

10.2 The contribution of small state law reform agencies to the development of the law

With adequate resources, law reform agencies in small states are able to make significant contributions to law reform.

For all these challenges, in a small state, a law reform agency does not have to be large or expensive to make a worthwhile contribution to the development of the laws of its country. It suffices that it has adequate resources put at its disposal and that it operates in an environment conducive to law reform. Reference to the publications referred to below can be found on the websites of the law reform agencies concerned.

In the Caribbean region, the Law Reform Commission of Trinidad and Tobago has made proposals for change in relation, for example, to the law on compensation for victims of crime, the law on computer misuse, adoption law, judicial review and the mechanisms for the protection of human rights. The Cayman Islands Law Reform Commission has recommended reforms for the development of the law with regard to, among other topics, landlord and tenant law, legal aid, the practice of law by legal practitioners, consumer protection law and contempt of court.

The Jersey Law Commission, with a very modest budget, has made proposals for reform of the law in relation to matters such as trust law (the rights of beneficiaries to information regarding a trust, the prohibition on trusts applying directly to Jersey immovable property), evidence (best evidence rule in civil proceedings, corroboration of evidence in criminal trials), law of *tutelles*, *dégrèvement*, law of real property, *voisinage*, law of contract, law on charities, law on security on immoveable property, law of partnership, bankruptcy, divorce, administrative redress and appeal against criminal convictions.

Law reform agencies in the Pacific Islands have been active in reviewing various aspects of the laws relating to their legal systems in order to respond to the needs of their societies. The Fiji Law Reform Commission has, since its establishment in 1979, made recommendations for changes to the law on aspects such as community-based alternatives to imprisonment, child abuse, duty solicitor scheme, abortion, drink driving, juvenile justice system, intellectual property and copyright, insurance, legal aid, solicitors trust accounts and legal practitioners fidelity fund, family law (divorce, affiliation, de facto relationships, maintenance, separation, custody and access, structure of family/domestic court), wills and succession, law regulating legal practitioners, criminal evidential rules (recent complaint, corroboration, confessions, competence and compellability, unsworn evidence, right to silence), bail, police powers, consumer protection, committal proceedings, liquor, bribery and corruption, prisons administration and domestic violence.

The Solomon Islands Law Reform Commission has, over the years, reviewed the Penal Code, and, also a matter of fundamental importance to the life of its people, the law on the land below the high water mark and the low water mark.

The Samoa Law Reform Commission has reviewed and recommended proposals for change on various aspects of its law: alcohol legislation, child care and protection legislation, civil procedure rules, commissions of inquiry legislation, coroners legislation, the Crimes Ordinance, the Criminal Procedure Act, laws relating to the judicial system (the District Court Act, the Judicature Ordinance), the law governing media regulation, legal practitioners legislation, national heritage legislation, prisons law, the Convention on the Elimination of all forms of Discrimination Against Women legislative compliance review, the law on the abuse of power by a paramount chief (*Pule a le Matai Saò*), sexual offenders' register legislation, the protection of Samoa's traditional knowledge and expressions of culture, and the Village Fono Act.

The Vanuatu Law Commission, which became operational only in 2011, has already considered dangerous drugs legislation, public health legislation, water legislation, the law on marriage and civil status registration, the Leadership Code Act and the Ombudsman Act.

The Papua New Guinea Constitutional and Law Reform Commission has, during the past 10 years, reviewed and submitted proposals for change on aspects of the law on the criminal justice system (committal proceedings, indictable offences triable summarily, the law on sorcery and sorcery-related killings, penalty provisions for criminal offences, laws on alcohol and drugs, review of district court practices and procedures), *ex parte* proceedings, proof of business and electronic records, incorporated land groups and the design of the system of voluntary customary land registration, environmental and mining laws relating to the management and disposal of tailings, and laws on the development and control of the informal economy, city planning and urban development.

The Commission has also reviewed the 'Implementation of the OLPG & LLG (Organic Law on Provincial Government and Local-level Government) on Service Delivery Arrangements: A Six Provinces Survey'.

In the African region, the Namibia Law Reform and Development Commission, which has recently celebrated 35 years of operation, has reviewed and recommended changes to various aspects of laws in order to enhance social justice and entrench a human rights culture in all spheres and aspects of the lives of Namibian citizens, uplift vulnerable communities (pre-independent Namibia was characterised by institutionalised discrimination, which was based on race, gender and some other forms of discrimination) and ensure that those that seek remedies for wrong-doing are appropriately assisted through various institutions and roles. Aspects reviewed relate to family law (including the status of married women, maintenance, marital property, divorce, succession and estates), domestic violence, rape, customary law, public gatherings, the electoral system, fisheries, criminal procedure, domestication of the United Nations Convention against Torture and other Cruel, Inhuman or Degrading Treatment or Punishment, administrative justice, insolvency law, traditional authorities in Ovambo communities, Government Institutions Pension Fund Legal Framework and the transformation of the Polytechnic of Namibia into the Namibia University of Science and Technology.

Many of the recommendations of the Namibian Commission have been implemented, such as the discriminatory concept of marital power, which was abolished by the Married Persons Equality Act; the recommendations arising from the Domestic Violence Project have been implemented; and the Combating of Rape Act and the Combating of Domestic Violence Act have been enacted, both aimed at combating violence against women.

The Mauritius Law Reform Commission, in 2006, after its reformation, embarked on a comprehensive review of Mauritian law and has submitted to the Attorney-General a significant number of reports and papers, with recommendations for change. The recommendations are aimed at:

- strengthening the rule of law, consolidating good governance and democracy, and reinforcing the human rights protection system;

- improving the judicial system, the operation of the legal profession and the provision of legal services;

- modernising the civil justice system;

- modernising the criminal justice system:

    - criminal investigation procedures;

    - law on bail;

    - rules as to disclosure;

    - rules as to costs;

    - criminal evidential rules;

    - effective handling of criminal cases; and

    - mechanism for the review of miscarriages of justice and for the correction of errors;

- renovating the criminal law in accordance with human rights norms and best international practices;

- modernising the Code Civil Mauricien:

    - law on persons and '*Droit extra-patrimonial de la famille*';

    - law on succession and matrimonial regimes ('*Droit patrimonial de la famille*');

    - law on obligations and specific contracts;

    - property law (including the law on '*co-propriété*');

    - law on '*sûretés*' and credit transactions;

    - law on prescription; and

    - aspects of private international law;

- improving the legal infrastructure for business:

    - reform of the Code de Commerce;

    - reform of the regulatory framework for the activities of real estate agents;

    - reform of the consumer protection regime; and

    - mediation and conciliation as mechanisms for settlement of disputes in commercial matters.

A significant proportion of the final recommendations of the Mauritius Law Reform Commission have been implemented:

- the recommendations contained in the report *Opening Mauritius to International Law Firms and Formation of Law Firms/Corporations* (May 2007);

- the recommendation contained in the report *Relationship of Children with Grandparents and other Persons under the Code Civil Mauricien* (June 2007);

- the recommendations in the report *Law on Divorce* (December 2008);

- the recommendations in the report *Bail and Related Issues* (Aug 2009);

- the recommendations and observations of the Commission in the report *Prevention of Vexatious Litigation* (October 2010) and in the opinion paper 'Appeal by Vexatious Litigant' (April 2011);

- the recommendations contained in the report *Crédit-Bail & Location Financière* (November 2011); and

- the recommendations contained in the report *Mechanisms for Review of Alleged Wrongful Convictions or Acquittals* (Nov 2012), which were partly approved and implemented.

Observations contained in reports/papers submitted by the Commission have also been taken into account by the legislature.

10.3 The structure and resources of law reform agencies in small states

10.3.1 Commissioners

As is common in standard model law reform agencies elsewhere, law reform agencies in small states and jurisdictions often include a member of the judiciary, often as the chair. When the Law Reform Commission of Mauritius was restructured in 2006, the previous lack of a judicial member was seen as a weakness, and was corrected in the new commission. Other members of the commissions are usually drawn from the ranks of practising lawyers and academia.

Some make provision for non-lawyer or lay members. An unusual feature of the membership of the Papua New Guinea Constitutional and Law Reform Commission is that it requires a member to have qualifications and experience in anthropology, sociology or political science. A similar provision exists in relation to the Solomon Islands Law Reform Commission.

It is a feature of small state and jurisdiction agencies that a number make provision for government law officers or other public sector lawyers to be members of the commission, such as in Mauritius, Lesotho and Namibia. In the Cayman Islands, there is no statutory obligation to do so, but it has become customary for the Solicitor General and the Director of Public Prosecutions to be appointed commissioners. The Constitutional and Law Reform Commission of Papua New Guinea is constituted by six prominent citizens: two are serving Members of Parliament, one has qualifications and experience in constitutional law, one has qualifications and experience in anthropology, sociology or political science, one is nominated by the Papua New Guinea Council of Churches to represent the Churches, and one is an *ex officio* member, namely the Dean of the Faculty of Law of the University of Papua New Guinea.

10.3.2 Staff

The viability and performance of a law reform agency is heavily dependent upon it having core personnel with a high degree of professional skills, committed to comparative legal research and able to engage meaningfully with stakeholders. It is important therefore that the Act establishing a law reform agency deals with staff matters and confers power to recruit personnel.

Retaining staff is a major challenge in small states.

In some small Commonwealth states, the Act establishing a law reform agency does not deal with staff matters, which can be a serious impediment to a law reform agency realising its mission. It may be difficult for the chair, or a commissioner, appointed on a part-time basis, to act also as a research officer.

In other small Commonwealth states, provision is made in the Act for the law reform agency to be assisted by officers and employees of the public service made available to it. This arrangement may be practical, but may turn out, on occasion, not to be satisfactory. For example, in Mauritius the Law Reform Commission, which was first established in 1992 and operated until 2006 when it was abolished and a new Commission set up, could not operate effectively because of the unavailability of staff:

The Commission at present does not have any staff. The Act envisaged that the Attorney-General's office would provide 'officers to assist the Commission in the discharge of its functions'. This has never materialised. The Commission understands that the Attorney-General's office is under heavy pressure as far as staffing is concerned and understands that it may not be in a position to delegate any officer to the Commission to assist it... The lack of staff seems to have been the major stumbling block to the proper operation of the Commission. Researching a theme, debating on it and writing up a report are all time consuming. It was not very realistic to have expected part-time members and a part-time Chairman to undertake the work in the absence of officers delegated by the Attorney-General's Office.[3]

In a number of small Commonwealth states, although the members of staff are public servants recruited by a public service commission or other equivalent body, provision is also made for the recruitment of personnel by the law reform agency. In small states, it is much to be preferred that the law reform agency be entrusted with the power to recruit personnel on such terms and conditions as it may think fit (having regard to pay grading in the public service and the need to recruit and retain competent personnel). This point was made in the report of the then Mauritius Law Reform Commission, *The Reform of the Law Reform Commission*, as a result of which the Commission was reconstituted.

The Samoa Law Reform Commission points to inadequate salaries as one reason for a lack of senior staff to support the Executive Director and Assistant Executive Director. The Commission also suffers a high rate of staff turnover, a serious problem for law reform projects, which, because of their nature, can be lengthy. The Commission relies on a volunteer for some policy and information and communications technology work, and on an unpaid short-term internship programme.

In order to enable a law reform agency to evolve into a strong institution, it is important that it should have high-level core personnel who can develop expertise in law reform and provide momentum over time. Members, who more often than not are part time, and will all, most likely, be at the law reform agency for a relatively short determinate term of office, are unlikely to be able to provide that sort of momentum.

Staff must be managed, supervised and given a sense of direction. It is therefore not uncommon for Acts establishing law reform agencies to make provision for the appointment of a chief executive, secretary or similar officer to lead the staff.

A lack of resources and limited professional networks may also mean that the adequate training of staff is a problem.

There may be options for innovative approaches to staffing that small state and jurisdiction law reform agencies could explore. It may be possible, for instance, to secure government commitment to allowing staff lawyers from the attorney-general's office to work for the agency for a defined number of hours per week. Such an arrangement may provide useful career experience for the member of staff, and allow them to undertake a more interesting and varied range of work. That in turn might help the attorney-general's office to retain staff.

Similarly, it may be possible for the law reform agency to agree partnership arrangements with universities. It may be possible, for instance, for a doctoral candidate to work part time on a project that was directly relevant to their thesis. Alternatively, a member of staff of a law school might offer assistance, if in doing so they could expect to write an article for an academic journal on the strength of the experience.

10.3.3 Consultants and other specialists

A law reform agency in a small state may be called upon to review aspects of the law requiring specialised knowledge, and in respect of which members and staff may not have the required expertise. Most of the law reform agencies in small Commonwealth states have been conferred the power to recruit consultants for any of their projects.

Mauritius: Use of outside experts

According to the Mauritius Law Reform Commission Act 2005, the Commission may engage, on such terms and conditions as it may determine, persons with suitable qualifications and experience as consultants to the Commission. Pursuant to the Act, Robert Louis Garron, Professeur Honoraire at the Faculty of Law of the University of Aix-Marseille, has been working for the Commission as Law Reform Consultant for the reform of the Code Civil Mauricien, the Code de Commerce and the Code de Procédure Civile. Professor Romain Ollard, Vice-Doyen of the Faculty of Law of the University of Réunion, is currently providing assistance on an *ad hoc* basis as consultant for the reform of the Criminal Code.

Law reform agencies also have the power to establish an advisory committee or panel for advising and assisting it during any particular project, which may consist of persons having specialised knowledge in, or particularly affected by, the matter to be studied.

10.3.4 Funding and operational capacity

Funding is challenging in all jurisdictions, but especially in small states.

The operating expenses of law reform agencies in small states are met by annual budgetary allocations provided by parliament, with provision being made for them to be able to benefit from donor assistance. Funding is a critical issue for any law reform agency, but the difficulties may be magnified in small states and jurisdictions, which are typically developing countries with limited resources (perhaps with the exception of a small number that are established financial centres).

Funding must be sufficient to enable the agency to effectively discharge its mission with competent and motivated staff operating in a conducive environment (adequate office space with the required logistics). The Samoa Law Reform Commission's budget is monitored by the Ministry of Finance. Although there is adequate funding to carry out the Commission's work, greater investment is needed to ensure that the work of the Commission is effectively carried out, especially in relation to raising awareness, conducting public consultations and office space. The Commission currently does not have access to any online subscription legal services.

The potential difficulties were graphically illustrated by Dr Guy Powles, a lawyer and judge with experience of the Pacific region, who has written that

> *There appears to be a lack of appreciation on the part of finance ministers and treasury officials that law reform requires more than a lawyer and a computer... in the absence of adequate funding and personnel, it is difficult for full consideration to be given to law reform techniques and processes.*[4]

While aid funding clearly has a place, it is important that small state and jurisdiction law reform agencies are able to educate the relevant financial authorities of the need for reasonable and stable funding.

10.4 Functions and methodology

As with law reform agencies elsewhere, the law reform agencies in small Commonwealth states and jurisdictions are mandated to review the law and to make recommendations for reform. Also like other law reform agencies, the statutory provisions setting out the functions of the law reform agencies are often based on the United Kingdom's Law Commissions Act.

In some states, such as Namibia, Papua New Guinea, the Solomon Islands and Vanuatu, law reform agencies are tasked with reviewing customary law, or harmonising it with statute and common law. The Vanuatu Law Commission, exceptionally, is empowered to submit comments on any bill before the legislature.

The Commission in Papua New Guinea was formed by the amalgamation of a Law Reform Commission (which had become inactive) with the Constitutional Development Commission to form the Papua New Guinea Constitutional and Law Reform Commission. As a result, it is required to review the workings of the constitution, as well as to undertake law reform.[5]

The statutory provisions relating to the initiation of law reform projects are similar to those of other law reform agencies, as is the practice of relations between governments and commissions.

In some instances, law reform agencies are also requested, when making recommendations for reform, to prepare draft legislation (see Chapter 8). There is express reference to such a possibility in the legislation of the Namibian and Mauritian Commissions. Although there is no express provision in the Samoa Law Reform Commission Act 2008, the Commission in practice sometimes attaches draft bills to its reports; for example, a draft bill was attached to the final report on the reform of the Sex Offenders' Register.

The working methodology of small state law reform agencies is, again, similar to that adopted by other law reform agencies, as set out in this guide.

There is a particular commitment by small state and jurisdiction law reform agencies to comparative legal research. This arises both from a desire to evaluate the merits and demerits of the state's law in light of the experience of other

In addition to the usual functions, law reform agencies in some small states are mandated to review customary law.

Comparative legal research is of particular value to small states. As always, care must be taken to adapt lessons to the local context.

Vanuatu on the approach to comparative law research

Vanuatu is one of the smallest Commonwealth states, with a population of under 300,000 and a land area of 12,000 km².

In his presentation at the Australasian Law Reform Agencies Conference 2008 'The Birth and Rebirth of Law Reform Agencies: The Establishment of the Vanuatu Law Commission', Mr Al Kalsakau, Attorney-General of Vanuatu, emphasised the importance of care in the use of comparative research:

> *New laws in all jurisdictions are often inspired by foreign experiences... in developing countries 'legal transplants' or imported laws are common practice. Whilst well intentioned, donors and law reformers need to avoid the trap of drafting new laws to effect change and overcome loopholes or deficiencies with current systems without fully appreciating and understanding the role of custom traditions and the way institutions and enforcement agencies function and are resourced. New laws do not solve problems simply by virtue of the fact they exist, and laws and regulations that are overly complex or fail to take local context into account will not be effective and can in fact create more problems than they solve.[6]*

jurisdictions, and from a conviction that the laws of a small state should reflect best international practices. Concomitant to this is an understanding that legal transplants must be made to adapt to the local context. Laws must reflect and advance a country's social and economic interests. A law reform agency would have to be mindful of avoiding importing 'models' and transplanting laws that are inconsistent with national legal, customary and socio-economic norms.

For small state and jurisdiction law reform agencies, consultation is no less significant than for other law reform agencies, and may indeed be more so. Small states have known their share of political conflict, and as Mr M Qetaki, Executive Chairman of the Fiji Law Reform Commission, has said:

> *Without consultation, without engagement with the law reform process, there can be no sense by the community of the relevance of the laws to their way of life and the importance of the rule of law in their day-to-day business. Without this engagement there is always the potential for conflict and political upheaval.[7]*

The result is that, for all the challenges they face, small state and jurisdiction law reform agencies have made substantial contributions to the law for which they are responsible for reform.

10.5 Co-operation and regional law reform initiatives

A law reform agency in a small state stands to benefit from co-operation with other law reform agencies in its region or across the Commonwealth in order to tap the wealth of experience that other law reform agencies have. Despite great variation between law reform agencies, the features that law reform agencies have in common are more important than their differences. They have the same core functions and they experience very similar successes and difficulties.

It clearly makes sense for a law reform agency in a small state when reviewing an area of law to consider any reviews of that area that have been conducted elsewhere. Having made due allowance for all the differences between the jurisdictions and the factors surrounding the area of law, a law reform agency can often find extremely useful ideas in the reports of another law reform agency. The experience of other law reform agencies on methods and best practices about the manner in which the law reform process could be carried out can also be of great assistance.

Participation in both formal and informal international associations of law reform agencies is valuable for all law reform agencies, but particularly so for small state and jurisdiction agencies. The two more formal associations are the Commonwealth Association of Law Reform Agencies and the Association of Law Reform Agencies of Eastern and Southern Africa (see Appendix 2).

A law reform agency in a small state may find it advantageous to participate in a regional body or to develop twinning arrangements with larger law reform agencies.

More informally, there are close links between the Australian, New Zealand and Pacific agencies, arising from the conferences organised from time to time under the banner of the Australasian Law Reform Agencies Conference.

A law reform agency in a small state may find it advantageous to develop twinning arrangements with larger law reform agencies; mutual support can be particularly helpful when facing new trends or difficulties. Interaction with other law reform agencies by way of visits, exchanges, secondments and internships may prove valuable for the capacity building of a law reform agency.

Involvement in regional arrangements would also be very helpful, such as membership of the associations described in Appendix 2 below.

A law reform agency in a small state also needs to be involved in regional law reform initiatives if there is great potential for such development in its region; this is the case particularly in the Caribbean and the Pacific regions.

Notes

1   Jamaica has a Legal Reform Department located within government. The Jersey Law Commission is unusual in having all part-time and unpaid commissioners.

2   [LMSCJ (07)11], presented at Meeting of Law Ministers and Attorneys General of Small Commonwealth Jurisdictions, 4–5 October 2007, Marlborough House, London.

3   Pages 18–19 of report of the Law Reform Commission of Mauritius (2004).

4   G Powles, 'Challenge of Law Reform in Pacific Island States', in B Opeskin and D Weisbrot (eds), *The Promise of Law Reform* (Federation Press, Sydney, 2005), p 414.

5   Ibid, pp 414–415.

6   http://www.paclii.org/other/conferences/2008/ALRAC/Papers/Session%202/Session%202%20(Kalsakau).pdf

7   Mr M Qetaki, 'Law Reform in the Pacific Area, quoted in G Powles, 'Challenge of Law Reform in Pacific Island States', in B. Opeskin and D. Weisbrot (eds), *The Promise of Law Reform* (Federation Press, Sydney, 2005), p 421.

Appendix 1

Commonwealth Law Reform Agencies and Other General Law Reform Entities

Appendix 1
Commonwealth Law Reform Agencies and Other General Law Reform Entities

Name of country	Website
Australia	Australian Law Reform Commission http://www.alrc.gov.au
	Australian Capital Territory Law Reform Advisory Council http://www.justice.act.gov.au
	New South Wales Law Reform Commission http://www.lawreform.justice.nsw.gov.au
	Northern Territory Law Reform Committee http://www.justice.nt.gov.au/attorney-general-and-justice/law/ nt-law-reform-committee
	Queensland Law Reform Commission http://www.qlrc.qld.gov.au
	South Australian Law Reform Institute http://law.adelaide.edu.au/research/law-reform-institute
	Tasmania Law Reform Institute http://www.utas.edu.au/law-reform
	Victorian Law Reform Commission http://www.lawreform.vic.gov.au
	Law Reform Commission of Western Australia http://www.lrc.justice.wa.gov.au
Bahamas	Bahamas Law Reform and Law Revision Commission http://www.bahamas.gov.bs
Bangladesh	Bangladesh Law Commission http://www.lawcommissionbangladesh.org/
Canada	Alberta Law Reform Institute http://www.alri.ualberta.ca
	British Columbia Law Institute http://www.bcli.org
	Manitoba Law Reform Commission http://www.manitobalawreform.ca
	Law Reform Commission of Nova Scotia http://www/.lawreform.ns.ca
	Law Commission of Ontario http://www.lco-cdo.org
	Law Reform Commission of Saskatchewan http://www.lawreformcommission.sk.ca

Name of country	Website
Cayman Islands	Cayman Islands Law Reform Commission http://www.lawreformcommission.gov.ky
Cyprus	Office of the Law Commissioner olcommissioner@olc.gov.cy
Dominica	Dominica Law Revision Commission http://www.justice.gov.dm
Falkland Islands	Falkland Islands Law Commissioner http://www.fig.gov.fk/legal/index.php/law-commissioner
Fiji	Fiji Law Reform Commission http://www.ag.gov.fj
Ghana	Ghana Law Reform Commission http://www.mojagd.gov.gh/law-reform-commission Lagos State Law Reform Commission http://www.lawrecom.lg.gov.ng
India	Law Commission of India http://lawcommissionofindia.nic.in/
Jamaica	Legal Reform Department, Ministry of Justice http://www.moj.gov.jm/legal-reform
Kenya	Kenya Law Reform Commission http://www.klrc.go.ke
Lesotho	Law Reform Commission of Lesotho http://www.llrc.gov.ls
Malawi	Malawi Law Commission http://www.lawcom.mw
Malaysia	Law Revision and Law Reform Division http://www.agc.gov.my
Malta	Malta Law Revision Commission
Mauritius	Law Reform Commission of Mauritius http://lrc.govmu.org
Namibia	Law Reform and Development Commission http://www.lawreform.gov.na
New Zealand	New Zealand Law Commission http://www.lawcom.govt.nz/
Nigeria	Nigerian Law Reform Commission http://www.nlrc.com.ng/
Pakistan	Law and Justice Commission of Pakistan http://www.ljcp.gov.pk/
Papua New Guinea	Papua New Guinea Constitutional and Law Reform Commission http://www.paclii.org/pg/lawreform/clrc-index.html
Rwanda	Rwanda Law Reform Commission http://www.rlrc.gov.rw
Samoa	Samoa Law Reform Commission http://www.Samoalawreform.gov.ws
Sierra Leone	Sierra Leone Law Reform Commission www.lawrefcom.sl

Name of country	Website
Singapore	Singapore Legislation and Law Reform Division http://www.agc.gov.sg
Solomon Islands	Solomon Islands Law Reform Commission http://www.paclii.org/sb/lawreform/SBLawRComm/ http://www.paclii.org/gateway/LRC/SILRC/index.shtml
South Africa	South African Law Reform Commission http://www.Salawreform.justice.gov.za
Sri Lanka	Law Commission of Sri Lanka http://www.lawcom.gov.lk
Tanzania	Law Reform Commission of Tanzania http://www.lrct.go.tz Zanzibar Law Review Commission http://www.zanjustice.go.tz http://zanjustice.org.tz
Trinidad and Tobago	Law Reform Commission of Trinidad and Tobago http://www.ag.gov.tt
Uganda	Uganda Law Reform Commission http://www.ulrc.go.ug/
United Kingdom	Law Commission for England and Wales http://www.lawcom.gov.uk/ Scottish Law Commission http://www.scotlawcom.gov.uk Jersey Law Commission http://www.jerseylawcommission,org
Vanuatu	Vanuatu Law Commission http://www.lawcommission.gov.vu
Zambia	Zambia Law Development Commission www.zldc.org.zm/

Appendix 2

Associations of Law Reform Agencies

Appendix 2
Associations of Law Reform Agencies

The Commonwealth Association of Law Reform Agencies

Approximately half of all Commonwealth countries have law reform agencies. The Commonwealth Association of Law Reform Agencies was established in 2003/2004 to encourage, facilitate and take forward co-operative initiatives in law reform. It is committed to the Commonwealth's values, and received formal accreditation to the Commonwealth in 2005, and has received annual re-accreditation ever since. The Commonwealth Association of Law Reform Agencies provides capacity-building support for law reform internationally, for law reformers in government and for those working in law reform agencies.

The Commonwealth Association of Law Reform Agencies has a broad set of objectives in its constitution.

Some of the Commonwealth Association of Law Reform Agencies' activities are listed below:

- The Commonwealth Association of Law Reform Agencies organises international conferences on law reform, in partnership with the national law reform agency in the jurisdiction. They take place immediately before or after the Commonwealth Law Conferences, in the same country as the Conference. They have been arranged ever since 2005, in alternate years.

- The Commonwealth Association of Law Reform Agencies provides training about good practice in law reform. Some training is in-country; other training is regional or international.

- The Commonwealth Association of Law Reform Agencies has drafted this guide to good practice in law reform, as a joint production with the Commonwealth Secretariat.

- The Commonwealth Association of Law Reform Agencies engages with the Commonwealth and with governments to seek high-quality law reform geared to the specific country, including (1) by encouraging and assisting the establishment and development of effective and good-quality law reform agencies, both inside and outside the Commonwealth; and (2) by being significantly involved in triennial Commonwealth Law Ministers Meetings since 2005, both those attended by the law ministers of all Commonwealth countries and those attended by the law ministers of small Commonwealth jurisdictions.

• The Commonwealth Association of Law Reform Agencies has developed strong relationships with many relevant organisations, including as a founder member of the Commonwealth Legal Forum, a group of Commonwealth legal associations, including the Commonwealth Association of Legislative Counsel, Commonwealth Lawyers Association, Commonwealth Legal Education Association, Commonwealth Magistrates and Judges Association, the British Institute of International and Comparative Law and the Commonwealth Secretariat.

• The Commonwealth Association of Law Reform Agencies undertakes other law reform activities, such as giving advice and assistance, and conducting reviews of existing law reform machinery and methods.

Membership of the Commonwealth Association of Law Reform Agencies is generally open to:

• institutional law reform agencies;

• individuals with a current or previous tie to a law reform agency; and

• other bodies and individuals supporting the aims of the Commonwealth Association of Law Reform Agencies.

Most members are from the Commonwealth. However, the Commonwealth Association of Law Reform Agencies also has members from outside the Commonwealth, who are also most welcome.

WEBSITE: www.calras.org

The Association of Law Reform Agencies of Eastern and Southern Africa

This association was formed in 2003. Its members are the law reform agencies and entities in some 14 countries in eastern and southern Africa.

Its purposes, as detailed in its constitution, are to:

- exchange and share ideas on best practices in law reform;

- exchange and share ideas on the development of law within the countries of the member agencies in accordance with the principles of human rights, good governance and the rule of law; and

- collectively contribute to the attainment of the objectives of member agencies.

WEBSITE: www.justice.gov.za/alraesa

The Federation of Law Reform Agencies of Canada

This Federation was formed in 1990. Its members are the five law reform agencies of Canada.

Its objectives are to:

- advance law reform in Canada;

- encourage the growth of co-operation among law reform agencies;

- educate the public on the role of law reform agencies; discuss and promote issues of interest and concern to law reform agencies;

- provide a forum for meetings of persons engaged with or interested in law reform;

- encourage professional self-development; and

- co-operate with other organisations that tend to promote the objects of the Federation.

WEBSITE: www.folrac.com

Australasian Law Reform Agencies Conference

These conferences have been held regularly since 1973. They are held every two years in different countries in Australasia.

The host country is responsible for establishing the theme for each conference. In recent years, these have included:

- in 2016, 'Law Reform – Survival and Growth' hosted by the Victorian Law Reform Commission;

- in 2014, 'The challenges of Law Reform in the Pacific' hosted by the Samoa Law Reform Commission;

- in 2012, 'Conversations about Law Reform – Sharing Knowledge and Experience' hosted by the Australian Capital Territory Law Reform Advisory Committee; and

- in 2010 'Law Reform –Relationships and the Future' hosted by the Queensland Law Reform Commission.

Index

Index